# More Ghosts
# of
# Upstate South Carolina

John Boyanoski

Shelor & Son Publishing, LLC

ISBN 13: 978-0-9761460-2-5
ISBN 10: 0-9761460-2-9

Library of Congress Control Number:   2008931142

Cover photograph by Derik and Jonathan Shelor
Cover design by Bill May and Stellar Studios

Shelor & Son Publishing, LLC
312 Fairmount Terrace
Mountville, PA  17554

www.SHELORandSON.com

1 2 3 4 5 6 7 8 9 0

For Shonda and Hannah

# Contents

# Acknowledgments

I would like to once again thank my wonderful family, who liked to share ghost stories with me when I was a child. Somehow, I don't think any of us foresaw my becoming a ghost writer. I would like to single out my cousin, Brandon Boyanoski, because—as he has reminded me many times since I wrote the first book—it was he who joined me on various ghost hunts through the mountains of Northeast Pennsylvania in search of such haunts at the Suscon Screamer.

My wife, Shonda, was invaluable when writing this book. She often served as my test audience as I did interviews over the phone from our kitchen table. I could tell if the story was going to be scary based on her reactions, which ranged from raised eyebrows to mouth agape shock. A really good story would lead to a flurry of questions from her as soon I finished the interview.

I also would like to thank all of the people who answered my many questions about the supernatural as I put this book together. Your input, insights, and advice helped make this a truly scary source for Upstate ghost legends.

# The Ghost on the Square
## Greenwood Hotel Has More
## Than Just Great Service

Some people get buyer's remorse pretty quickly after purchasing a property. They don't like it. It's the wrong color. It will take more money to restore than they originally expected. And people really couldn't have blamed John Huffman for feeling that way when he purchased the Inn on the Square, which is located in downtown Greenwood, in January 2005. The hotel was pretty run-down. Huffman fired most of the staff because he didn't think they were up to the task of turning the business around, but one longtimer who wasn't quite up to snuff stuck around. As Huffman would soon find out, he had a ghost that was quite unusual.

"It's one thing to be haunted," Huffman said. "But I have probably the world's most defective ghost."

"Bill," as he has come to be dubbed for no other reason than it sounded good, is quite a character, Huffman said. He can't walk through locked doors (or at least doesn't like to), he likes watching the Weather Channel, he prefers Scotch, and he gets a little testy when things don't go his way. And while Bill is the most recognized ghost at the Inn on the Square, he is not the only one. There have been at least three ghosts spotted on the third floor, and another "thing" that once made its presence known in the lobby, much to the annoyance of a clerk, who quit on the spot, and later another clerk refused to work the late shift ever again.

It is not uncommon to find a haunted hotel, inn, or bed and breakfast in the Upstate. They seem to be almost everywhere. Something about the semi-transiency of people coming in and out over the decades just seems to attract ghosts. In many cases, the lodgings can trace their ghost stories back generations, as the buildings have long provided temporary shelter for visitors.

The Inn on the Square is a little different. The yellowish-tan building is located on the edge of Uptown Greenwood. The inside has all the comforts of a modern three-star hotel, but also that certain regalness of a classic downtown hotel, with an authentic English pub and ornate moldings in the lobby. Looks can be deceiving. Huffman said the original buildings date back to the early part of the twentieth century. Yes, buildings with an "s." It originally was a two-story building with an adjoining one-story structure. A small alley split the two. At least seventeen businesses were located in the buildings over the years, including a funeral home, a grocery store, a furniture store, and a garage. The buildings went vacant in the 1970s and began to deteriorate. In the late 1970s and early 1980s, there was a major push to revitalize Greenwood, and one of the plans called for a new hotel. It wasn't until 1985, though, that two local developers were able to make it happen. They got the city to condemn the alley, then united the buildings and opened a forty-eight-room hotel. The hotel's lobby is located where the alley used to be. Eventually, though, new out-of-town owners purchased the property and let it fall into disrepair.

That is where Huffman and his wife, Misty, came into the picture. He had retired from the real estate business to do some writing, and she decided it might be fun to open a bed and breakfast. Huffman asked some of his former real estate associates to keep their eyes open for a good place in the Upstate. Someone recommended the Inn on the Square. It was much bigger than a B&B, but offered much better value down the road. Huffman checked it out, and despite the problems with staff and the building's appeal, he saw the potential and purchased it in 2005 with the idea of renovating.

However, he may have had second thoughts two weeks after buying it. He was staying on the third floor of the hotel and working pretty much nonstop. One night, he was sitting at the bar in the hotel's pub talking to the female bartender. It was around midnight and no one else was there. He decided they should just close up. They turned off the lights and closed the two very large wooden doors that lead into the bar. The bartender stopped to talk to the night clerk, and Huffman got on the elevator to go to his room. The third floor opens up over the atrium, and as he glanced down he could only see the clerk and the bartender sitting in some chairs chatting. No one else was there. His feet only had to shuffle a few more steps and he would be in his room and done for the day.

BAM-BAM-BAM-BAM-BAM-BAM!

The noise jerked Huffman out of his daze. He leaned over the railing to look down into the lobby. The bartender and desk clerk were on their feet staring at the bar's large doors. The clerk hollered up that Huffman must have locked "Bill" in the bar.

Huffman headed for the elevator, wondering who Bill was and how come he had not seen him just a few minutes before. He got back to the first floor after punching the numbers frantically, and strode across the tiled lobby. He pulled his keys from his pocket and turned the lock. The doors swung open on their own with a gust of air that blew the hairs on his arms. Huffman said it was almost like a sonic boom in force. And when Huffman flicked on the lights, no one was there. He turned to the night clerk and asked who and where Bill was, and the night clerk told him that Bill was the resident ghost. Huffman was incredulous. Ghosts, if they are real, should be able to get through a locked door, he said. Not Bill, he was told. Bill didn't like being locked in the bar.

"Of all the luck," Huffman thought, "don't tell me I have a defective ghost as well."

Huffman relocked the doors, went upstairs, and thankfully nothing else happened. At least not that night.

3

Huffman would soon learn a lot about Bill and his prankish ways, which run from simply juvenile to downright mean. Huffman has spent more than $600,000 on renovations, which apparently have not been to Bill's liking. He has caused leaks in the walls when no water pipes were busted. He has torn up the bar and ripped a television off the wall.

"He can be very destructive when he is all wound up," Huffman said.

But he has a playful side as well. He flickers lights around the bar and likes to make noises when no one else is there. All of the waitstaff pin their aprons to their clothes because Bill likes to untie their knots while the employees are taking orders. A fun game for regulars at the inn's Fox and Hound bar is to look for the person Bill decides to tap on the shoulder. Regulars know about Bill's game, and don't pay heed. A newcomer doesn't and naturally reacts to the tap and turns their head to see who is there. The crowd breaks out in laughter at Bill's victim, who is then let in on what just happened.

And while the bar was once where the chapel was located when the building was a morgue, that has not stopped Bill from knocking down a different kind of spirit from time to time. One night another female bartender was working by herself and the main doors were closed. It was getting close to last call and no one was in the bar when she looked up to see an elderly, very distinguished man with gray hair and wearing a crisp, three-piece gray suit sitting at the end of the bar. She went over to get his order. He politely asked for a scotch and water. She soon mixed the drink in an ice-filled tumbler and brought it to the man, then walked to the other end of the bar to get the man's tab going. When she turned back around to look at him, he was gone, but the untouched drink was on the bar. Her eyes scanned across the room, but no one was there. She looked at the doors. She hadn't heard them budge. The bartender quickly went to the desk clerk in the lobby. Had an elderly man just walked by? No.

The girl quit the next day, Huffman said.

Bill soon showed another odd habit that Huffman and others would experience at various times. They would be watching television in the bar, and the wine cellar door would swing open. This is a very heavy door that really has to be pushed to get open. It would take an extremely powerful wind to open it on its own, and no breezes were ever felt when it happened. Then the television's screen would start flipping until it got to the Weather Channel. Then, most eerie of all, a chair in front of the television would turn around to face the set. Huffman was telling this story one slow evening to some friends at the bar, but the bartender was a skeptic. He kept saying it was a hoax or the child of an overactive imagination. The bartender had made this rant before, and Huffman said Bill was going to get him one day. The bartender kept saying there was no ghost. Just then, the cellar door flew open, the television changed stations, and the chair changed directions. Huffman pointed to that as proof and his guests looked on in amazement, but the bartender still was in doubt. He said it was somehow a trick and that the whole thing was akin to something male cows leave in grassy fields.

Just then a small, metal door from one of the refrigerators came sailing across the bar and hit the bartender in the leg. It was a small door, but it weighed about forty pounds and had been ripped from the hinges. The man quit immediately.

With all of this going on, Huffman wondered if Bill was making the rounds on the third floor as well. One of his cleaning ladies refused to go on the third floor, but wouldn't tell him why. She said she would do anything he asked of her, but don't send her to that floor. Huffman also noticed that some guests would stay on the third floor, but then come down to get a new room during the night. They would give evasive answers as to why they wanted to leave their room, but insisted it be on a different floor. They too wouldn't say what had scared them.

Finally, a woman came down one morning and called for the manager. Now, it's never a good thing when someone calls for the manager at a hotel, and Huffman went to the front with a sense of dread. The woman introduced herself and said she was a psychic. She asked if he knew the hotel was haunted. He replied affirmatively. Maybe she felt he was a little too glib and intoned that she was serious. Huffman looked back at her and said so was he and mentioned some of Bill's antics. The woman smiled, and said Bill was not alone. She told Huffman that she and her husband were lying in bed in one of the third-floor rooms when she awoke around 3 a.m. There at the foot of the bed was an elderly woman, a younger woman, and a child. They just stared at the hotel guest before they vanished. The psychic also said she felt the presence of an older, distinguished gentleman, but did not see him.

Huffman quickly realized this may have been the reason the one maid wouldn't go on the third floor. Some of the maids later said they, too, had seen the distinguished man walking along the third floor. When they got close to him, he would vanish into thin air. The maids also reported things such as someone unraveling all of the toilet paper in locked rooms, which they soon attributed to the ghosts. Huffman kept the story of the three ghosts to himself, but soon another person would confirm it. A young woman who liked to sing karaoke at the bar stayed at the hotel one night. She had never claimed to see ghosts before, but told the staff that she had seen three figures standing in her room that morning. When she tried to get a better look, they were gone. The young woman would return to the bar, but would never sleep in a room there again.

"That scared the hell out of her," Huffman said.

Bill, though, apparently didn't want to be upstaged by the third-floor ghosts and decided to make himself more of a known entity. A popular band played the bar one night and the local newspaper was there to cover it. Plenty of pictures were snapped, and Huffman looked forward to reading the article about his hotel the next day. The story was good, but there were no photos, which perplexed him. He called up the photo editor to see if there was a way he could get copies of the unused photos. The editor said there was a reason none of the

6

photos were used. Strange lights and blurs appeared in each of the photos, rendering then unusable for print. Two of the pictures showed flames inside the bar, which left the photographer completely perplexed.

Bill soon branched out into the world of video, as well. Huffman had begun installing cameras in various parts of the hotel for security reasons. Two of them were placed in the bar and were motion activated. After the night clerk described an unexplained disturbance in the bar after closing hours one night, Huffman went to the tapes.

The cameras captured images of the bar staff closing up, and the video went black with a 2:30 a.m. time stamp because no one was moving around the bar area. However, the camera behind the bar kicked back on at 4:54 a.m. At first nothing was visible in the frame, but soon a light started to build. That was followed by what looked like sparks coming from a campfire, and finally the sparks came together to form a lighted ball. That orb began thrashing around at high speeds behind the bar before whipping out of the view of the camera. At that point, the second camera picked up the motion. The ball could be seen flying around the restaurant and lounge area in the near complete darkness. Tables and chairs went flying out of the way as if a demolition derby were going on inside the room. The ball then made an abrupt turn and headed straight toward the camera lens. Just then, the two big doors on the other side of the room opened and the night clerk could be seen rushing in, frantically trying to figure out what was going on. And just over the clerk's shoulder, a gray man-like blur could be seen heading from the bar into the lobby. Bill strikes again?

The damage to the room was extensive, including a television ripped from the wall. Huffman was reduced to having a little chat with Bill one night. A couple of friends came over for a "séance" and did things such as drink some shots of tequila in Bill's honor, but then Huffman got down to brass tacks. He didn't mind Bill hanging around and playing little jokes. The violent side, however, was not welcome. If Bill didn't stop destroying equipment, he was going to get a real paranormalist in there and kick the ghost out to the street.

Since then, Bill has been mischievous, but not malevolent. As an added precaution, however, anyone closing up the bar at night yells out a little reminder to Bill that they are done for the evening and that he needs to leave as well. Thankfully, that has helped put an end to Bill's banging on the doors at night. Bill may be a defective ghost, but he knows the rules about closing time.

There is one last unexplained tale from the Inn on the Square. It started when Huffman was looking for the video image of a guest who had provided a false identification card when he had checked in the night before. The cameras would have gotten a good shot of the culprit. As he flipped through the speeding images, Huffman saw an employee talking to the desk clerk, and then something odd in the picture. He stopped the tape, rewound it, and played it back at normal speed. The first few images showed both people chatting, but then the face on the employee who was not behind the desk began to change. The eyes bulged and the tongue protruded. It took the shape of a gargoyle's mask. And as the man turned to walk away, the hideous visage remained suspended in midair just staring at the clerk until it simply vanished.

When Huffman showed the clerk the video and asked if anything odd had happened, the clerk simply walked out and never returned.

"It was very frightening," he said. "We haven't been able to explain it."

But another clerk had experienced problems while working the third shift as well. One morning Huffman came in to find the young woman's eyes swollen from crying all night. She said something—she believed it was Bill—had been playing tricks on her all night long. Things such as whispering unintelligible words in her ear and making walking noises across the floor. The young woman also said she had heard doors opening and closing through the wee hours of the morning. Unlike other employees who had bad experiences with the ghosts, the girl didn't quit. But she did refuse to work the overnight hours again.

Huffman has spent a lot of time researching the history of the building to see if he can figure out who his nonpaying guests might have been during their mortal lives. He can find no record of anyone dying or being killed on the premises. And while the property was a funeral home, those are places not often associated with ghosts because the dead tend to have found peace by the time they reach that stage or to stick around where they died. He is somewhat at a loss as to who Bill and his cohorts might be. And despite some of the more vicious pranks and the frightening gargoyle face that appeared in the lobby, Huffman doesn't seem like someone who is going to be scared off by ghosts. He knows Bill is a prankster and has come to appreciate the ghost to some extent.

Even if he is defective.

# Witches of Fairfield County
## What Really Happened to
## Mary Ingelman and Others in 1792?

The American legal system is filled with stories of great hero-
ics, tragedies, and injustices. The story of Mary Ingelman falls
into the third category. Almost a century after witch hysteria
gripped the Massachusetts colony based on the accusation of
teenage girls, an even more bizarre case erupted in what is now
Fairfield County, located just east of Newberry County, in 1792.
A woman named Mary Ingelman, along with three others, was
accused of witchcraft based on testimony that she made women
and cows levitate, attended a witch's convention, and turned
her grandson—among other people—into a horse. (Through no
record exists of the court dialogue, I can probably say for certain that the grandson, Jacob Free, did not testify that "I feel
much better now" after the eyes in the courtroom looked at his
human form in disbelief.) The story of Mary Ingelman has taken
on a somewhat ghastly legend, but the truth is much more real.

Origins for the tale of Mary Ingelman can be found in documents written by Phillip Edward Pearson sometime in the mid-
1800s. Pearson was a longtime prosecutor for the Middle Court,
which included Fairfield. His documents also mention the three
other accused witches—Sally Smith, a Mr. Haxler, and his wife—
but he focuses heavily on Ingelman, who was seventy years old
at the time and likely had been born in Germany. Or at least
she was of Germanic descent. It can be believed that Pearson

found the sad story of Ingelman and the others somewhere in his records. However, Will Kale, a Fairfield-based historic researcher, said that Pearson likely knew Ingelman directly. Kale identified Germanic runes located on Ingelman's chimney that are called an Ingwaz, which is a diamond-shaped figure associated with fertility and good fortune. The four people had moved to Fairfield from the Lexington County area and were said to be skilled in the use of herbs to help cure illnesses.

There is no other documentation of what happened to Ingelman and the other three in 1792, but she definitely was a real person, said Pelham Lyles, director of the Edgefield County Museum. Her husband is listed in U.S. Census documents, and their farm building existed for centuries in the southern part of Fairfield, just above Lexington County. Lyles later led an effort to save the log cabin, only to see it get moved to North Carolina at the last minute.

Kale said he found out about the Ingelman case shortly after moving to the county in 1999. He became intrigued with the idea that there were other witch trials outside of Salem, and said that this one was particularly gruesome. He now wonders how many other witch trials were undertaken during these years.

"I was surprised that this illegal trial took place where people were charged, found guilty, and tortured for things they clearly did not and could not do, like turn a person into a horse," he said.

Kale often compares the Ingelman case to the famed Salem witch trials that took place in 1692. That miscarriage of justice, which included the hanging of several people with mental handicaps, one woman's being accused of witchery because she had clean shoes, and the crushing of an elderly man underneath a pile of rocks, happened before there was a U.S. government in place to prevent illegal trials. The Ingelman trial, according to the Kale, was clearly illegal under the auspices of the then four-year-old U.S. Constitution because she was punished without due process.

According to the Pearson document, cattle became ill and people began to act possessed in Fairfield around 1792. That led to Ingelman and the three others' being accused of witchcraft. The case against Ingelman was truly bizarre and, as Kale said, hard to believe. One man said Ingelman put a spell on him and his sister that caused them to levitate and they could not be held down when four men tried to pull on them. Another said Ingelman had done the same thing to his two children. Then one of Ingelman's sons from her first marriage accused her of making one of his cows fly up into the air and break its neck when it fell back to the ground. That man's son accused Ingelman of turning him into a horse. However, it is stated that the youth only made the allegation under threat of torture. Like Kale said, this was a sham of a trial. Another person made the same claim of being turned into a horse, and then said Ingelman rode him to a "grand convention of witches." The devil was alleged to have been at this meeting, and when he complemented Ingelman on the horse, she explained it was really a man who had crossed her.

With that kind of evidence, a mob took Ingelman, Smith, and the Haxlers to the home of a man named Thomas Hill, a farmer who lived just south of Winnsboro. He was to serve as judge. Another man named Crossland was to act as executioner. Ingelman and the other three offered no defense to the accusations. It is possible they knew little English and therefore couldn't understand what was being said. They were then tied to the joists of the home and flogged. Their feet were then burned until only the bones were left. Amazingly, the four survived the horrific ordeal and were promptly let go.

However, Ingelman was walking home when she was attacked again by an unknown assailant. Left for dead, someone else came along the path the next day and saved her. Interestingly enough, Ingelman got a judge to make out an arrest warrant for Crossland. He was found guilty and fined five pounds. He never paid the fine, and was never heard from again.

Pearson's documents said Ingelman was a nice and decent old lady, who was born in Germany and knew a lot about herbal remedies. Perhaps people thought of her as a witch because of her medical skills, and maybe she made an enemy for some unknown reason along the way. That likely led to the bizarre tales and allegations that were brought against her.

Ingelman's name fades from history after that, and there is no record of when or where she died. However, her legend grew somewhat, but in a bad way, Kale said. In the early 2000s, he began hearing stories of Ingelman's having been hanged outside the courthouse, but saved before she died. He feels that story is doing a disservice to Ingelman.

"The truth about Mary Ingelman and what took place is much more interesting than the tall tales told about her in 1792 in an illegal trial and the new tall tales being fabricated about her today some 216 years later," he said.

# The Disgusting House
## One Family's Scary Tale from Greer and Beyond

Sarah B. (an alias, used at the homeowners' request) slumped down after a hard day of moving her belongings into a new home in Greer. It had been a long day of carrying boxes and furniture off of trucks and into the house. Her husband had driven back to Georgia to pick up the rest of their items, which left Sarah and her mother to unpack. It was around 1 a.m., and they cleared off some space on the couches to sleep for a few hours before the rest of the household wares arrived. Her eyes had barely shut when she heard a loud pounding coming from the other side of the house. She looked up to see if she had dreamt it, but her mother apparently had heard the noises, too. They turned on the lights and looked around the one-story structure, but didn't find anything. Sarah just shrugged it off as the house settling or maybe some pipes with water pushing through them.

"Looking back, I realized that the hauntings and strange things started on the first night we were there," she said.

Sarah and her husband moved into the house in 1998, but didn't know much about the previous owners. However, what they soon learned about them made them wonder if the strange things that were happening in the home may have been related. The man who lived in the home had been gunned down in cold blood in front of his family. The murder had occurred elsewhere, but it led the family to move.

Sarah said she began noticing strange things. An item would go missing and then show up minutes later in a place where they had just looked. She and her husband always felt uneasy inside the home, and would often snap at each for no real reason. They also got the feeling that they were being watched and that someone was always standing right behind them when they went from room to room.

At first they were willing to chalk up the bad feelings to living in a new home. However, one event would soon unnerve them. The couple had a custom of reading the Bible every night. They had one in particular that they had gotten from a visiting preacher, and it became a favorite. They went to get it one night, and it was gone. They always put it back in the same place, and there was no explanation as to how it could have gone missing. They searched the entire house and found nothing. Months went by, and the missing Bible made them wonder what was going on. Then one day Sarah decided it was time to put her infant daughter down for a nap. She grabbed a CD that played lullabies and brought it into the baby's room. Her child soon fell asleep and Sarah turned off the recording. She grabbed the disc and walked to the other room to put it away. She nearly jumped back in shock. There on top of the CD holder was the missing Bible. That was just the start.

A few days later, she was vacuuming and moved a trash can to empty it. When she returned, she noticed a large dent in the wall that hadn't been there a few seconds before. Thinking she just may have never noticed it before, she called her husband at work to see if he knew anything about it. Nothing. Sarah was beginning to feel a little uneasy, but kept cleaning. She moved a couch to vacuum behind it and noticed that one of the prongs on the lamps was completely bent to the side. The lamp had been working fine, but there was no way power should have been running through it in that condition.

That was when Sarah learned from a local news broadcast about the fate of the previous owner. The newfound knowledge did little to avail her fears, and the unusual events continued to increase in frequency. A friend came over one night, and they were talking in the kitchen. Sarah told her about the unexplained activity, and her friend said it was weird. Just then the lights flickered in the kitchen. Thinking it might have been a power surge, she called to her husband in the other room. Had the lights flickered in there? No, he replied. They waited a few minutes and nothing happened. Her friend mentioned the oddities again, and once again the lights flickered. Sarah quickly suggested they switch to a less haunted topic. Another night, Sarah was out in the front yard after having just gotten her daughter down for bed. She looked back at the house and could see her husband pacing back and forth in the living room. And then clear as a bell she saw him keep walking, but there appeared to be a skeleton remaining where he had been standing. The skeleton just stood there as she scanned her eyes across the house to find her husband. She saw him walk back in the room and the skeleton disappeared. One of their cats also acted panicky whenever in the house and would run among the rooms with its hair standing straight up.

"There was so much that happened," she said. "It's hard to remember it all."

The events, though, would soon go from odd to very scary. Sarah's daughter was getting older and started to talk. She began saying she saw a scary man in certain rooms, and would often refuse to play by herself. When Sarah tried to question the little girl, the child could only say that it was a "bad man" who scared her. That really bothered Sarah. Before, she wasn't sure if it was just a child's imagination or something else, such as fatigue or lighting, that made her see things. But after three years in the home, the family decided to move. They spent all day moving, and decided that the last trip of the night would be the final one ever. Anything that couldn't be loaded would be left behind. They pulled up in two cars, and noticed a black cloud of smoke seemingly enveloping the house. It didn't smell like fire, but it made everyone uneasy. As soon as Sarah opened the door to the car, her daughter started screaming. Nothing

Sarah could do would calm the child down. In desperation, she looked to her husband. There was something scaring their daughter. He would load up the car while she drove down the road and waited at a gas station. As soon as they got to the end of the driveway, her daughter's mood improved. She seemed to be relieved to be away from the house and asked where they were going. Her mother said down the road, and asked what the tantrum was all about. The child answered only that the house was disgusting. A short while later, her husband pulled up. He didn't want to be in the home any longer either.

"She could feel there was something not right," Sarah said.

A few months later, though, there was one more incident that scared Sarah greatly. Her daughter was playing with a deck of cards in their new home. She drew out a joker card that looked particularly sinister. Her daughter turned to her and said that the joker had been in their old home. Sarah asked her what she meant. The little girl said again that he had lived in their home.

"I threw that deck of cards out," she said.

Sarah believes that what happened in the house was definitely supernatural, and tied to the home. But at least one of her friends is convinced that the ghosts have been following Sarah for years. Sarah said she was in high school when she saw a dark spectral figure hovering over her sleeping sister. Her sister started to rasp and choke, and Sarah rushed from her bed to push the figure away. It blew away like mist. The event happened several times during the night, and Sarah was sure she wasn't dreaming or asleep when it happened. Lying in her bed, Sarah convinced herself that it had been the curtains she had seen and went to sleep. The first thing she realized when she awoke was that there were no curtains in the room.

And then, just a few years ago, Sarah experienced one more unexplained event. By now she had two daughters, and the girls were sharing a room. She was putting them to bed one night, and was lying next to the older one in bed. She heard a voice call out her daughter's name. She thought she might have been dreaming, but the voice also woke her daughter, who asked her mother who had called her name. She said it was her imagination, and soothed the child back to sleep. A short while later, she went to her husband, who was in the living room. Had he called their daughter's name or heard anything? He said no. That night their daughter crawled into their bed, saying she was scared. In the morning, the young girl said it wasn't a nightmare that had made her come to the room, but Sarah tried to get her daughter's attention focused elsewhere. The child dropped the subject, but after school she told her mother she had to tell her what had happened. Sarah relented. The daughter said someone had been tugging her covers and that when she sat up in bed something that felt like two hands ran down her back. It is those kinds of events that make her friend think that spirits are now following her, but Sarah hopes not.

"There are still some things we can't explain," she said.

# The Ghosts of Tillman Hall
# and Then Some
## Numerous Ghosts Haunt
## Historic Winthrop University

Angel Johnson was sitting at the bottom of the main stairwell that leads to the bell tower of Tillman Hall—the most recognizable landmark on the campus of Winthrop University in Rock Hill. It was around 2 a.m., and her team of paranormal investigators was wrapping up yet another jaunt into the three-story building in the middle of campus. She was talking quietly with one of the members of her ghost tracking team when they heard a door about two stories above them open and close. There was no way the wind could have moved the heavy wooden door, and they figured it was a member of her team investigating the bell tower.

The sound of footsteps coming down the stairs seemed like nothing, and then they heard a faint hello. A little odd that a member of her organization would be so tentative, but Johnson figured they were looking for her. It was late and they needed to get going. She got up to stretch her legs and wait for the unseen member of the team. The footfalls that she had heard so clearly before and expected to be getting louder as the person came down the stairs didn't register anymore. Had the person turned around? But if they had done that, then Johnson would have heard the door open and close once again.

"I just got real quiet," she recalled. "There was no way some-one could have gotten past us or went back through the doors without us noticing."

Johnson and her partner went outside to confirm what they believed was an interlude with a ghost. No one else had been inside for a while now. They had been the last two out. Johnson is convinced that she had had the rare experience of hearing a ghost without the aid of electronic equipment. Many times, ghost hunters using such equipment will pick up unexplained voices and noises that were not audible when people were standing around.

"That was probably the most real contact we have had," said Johnson, who is director of the Rock Hill Ghost Hunters.

But it is by far not the only thing ever seen or heard on the top floor of Tillman Hall. Dozens of hand-written notes done in ink, pencil, and even crayon tell the stories of encounters with the famed South Carolina governor Ben Tillman, who is better remembered in history as "Pitchfork Ben." Mind you, that is not some kind of Satanic connotation attached to his legend. Tillman gained the title after he somewhat jokingly threatened to poke President Grover Cleveland with said de-vice. Then again, based on Governor Tillman's reputation, it's possible that he would have jabbed the president if given the opportunity.

"He was somewhat of a bad man," Johnson said

Tillman, so the story and the legends and the jottings on the wall go, is said to still roam the halls of the building that bears his name. Tillman was the keynote speaker when the corner-stone for the building was laid in 1894, and was a main propo-nent of the school's construction. It is said that the governor's administration forced chain gang laborers to help build the edi-fice and was pretty rough on the workers. There are still stock-ades in the basement where the convict workers were kept. The main building was renamed after him in 1962, after a previous science building that bore his named was torn down. The new Tillman Hall is on the National Register of Historic Places.

Johnson surmised that Tillman was very strongly tied to the building. "He feels he owns it," she said. But she also said there are plenty of other potential specters roaming the halls. Those include the ghost of one of the prisoners still hauling wood beams down the hall, the law enforcement officer whose job was to mind them, a young woman in a dark blue wool suit, and D. B. Johnson, the school's first president.

"There is a lot energy left over in there," she said.

The school's administration takes a somewhat humorous view of the hauntings, said Judy Longshaw, a spokeswoman for Winthrop. The alumni office does ghost tours of the building around Halloween each year, and freely talks about the stories. There is a rather long script that the alumni office reads to people who want to take the tour. It includes other stops on campus, but more on that later.

The alumni office tells the story of a graduate student seeing a large African American with no shirt on carrying a stack of wood over his shoulder in the building's basement. She knew there was no construction going on, so she went to ask if he needed directions. As she neared him, the man walked through a wall. Other students have said they've seen a very large man lurking in the shadows on the top floor. He is seen wearing an "Indiana Jones" style hat, and is believed to be Clem Long, the school's first law enforcement officer and the man responsible for keeping tabs on the prisoners. Then there is the young lady in the blue suit, who is believed to be the spirit of a former student from the 1920s or 1930s. She, too, vanishes when people get close. And there is Johnson, who has been linked to numerous odd happenings. His office moved several times while he worked in the administration building. Therefore, his spirit is believed to be the entity that will often lock people in and out of their offices, thinking it is his own. He has also been said to be fascinated with technology, and will turn on computers and copy machines to get a better look at how they work.

And then there is Tillman.

Tillman was born in 1847 in Edgefield County, which is famed for being the birthplace of eleven South Carolina governors. He enlisted in the Confederate Army at the start of the Civil War, but an illness led to his losing his left eye in 1864. After the war, he rose to power as a backer of farmers' rights as well as a strict segregationist. (It should be noted that some historians claim that Tillman was nicknamed "Pitchfork Ben" because of his agrarian stances.) He was elected governor in 1890 despite having never been elected to any other public office, and his tenure was noted for the founding of Clemson University as well as Winthrop. It was also marred by a riot in Darlington over the sale of liquor and his push to disenfranchise blacks. He was elected to the U.S. Senate in 1894 and served until his death in 1918. During the time, he was censured for assaulting fellow senator John L. McLaurin in 1902 and fought with the Department of the Navy over that agency's growing budget. After his death, he was buried in the Ebenezer Cemetery back in his hometown of Trenton.

With a record like that, Longshaw points out one interesting fact. Of all of the places that Tillman lived and worked, there is no real reason for him to haunt a college building in Rock Hill, even if the building was named after him. If anything, it should be students who would have the motive to haunt him. In 1906, he tried to prevent Winthrop students from returning home for Christmas. He labeled the idea a "distraction."

"Why would he be here?" she said laughingly. "He has no really overt connection."

It should also be noted that there is a Tillman Hall on the Clemson University campus, and old Ben has managed to stay away from that building. Yet, Longshaw admits that many employees say there is something not quite right about the building. People talk about unexplained chills in the air and seeing shadows that seem to dart along just out of eyesight. Or doors that were sure to be locked and are later found to be unlocked with no explanation. It is also said that he likes to keep tabs on the custodial staff by leaving notes on dusty tables and floors in order to make sure they get cleaned soon.

And then there is the very dark and foreboding portrait of Tillman that greets all visitors as they enter the main lobby. It is painted from the side view so that only half of Tillman's face is visible. The lone dark eye seems to follow people as they enter the building, though this is really due to the artistic style as opposed to any forces from beyond the grave. It was painted by famed artist Clara Barrett Strait, whose estate donated forty-eight portraits and $8,000 to the college upon her death in 1948. Yet, the Tillman portrait is not listed as one of those paintings. Longshaw said the school commissioned her to create the portrait, and bought it separately from the rest of the works. It should be noted that the portrait is hung close to the cornerstone whose laying was presided over by Tillman.

Michelle Mayes of the Palmetto Paranormal Research Group said it is still a very creepy picture.

"It just looks like it follows you across the room," she said.

Mayes's group also has done investigations into the building, but she said they did not pick up as much as paranormal activity as they expected. They snapped several pictures that show "orbs," those glowing balls that sometimes appear inexplicably in pictures taken inside haunted places. Still, she doesn't discount all of the reports of unexplained activity. The words scrawled on the walls make sure of that.

"I think it's a great place to investigate," she said.

Johnson said there is likely more spectral activity going on in the building than just Tillman. She feels there are more spirits hanging out in the area behind the auditorium, but investigators tend to focus more on the bell tower area because that is the section the Tillman stories are mainly associated with. Another area that her group feels carries some paranormal potential is the stockade in the basement. That is where the prisoners were kept during the building's construction. When her group investigated the stockade area, they picked up a large electromagnetic spike on their equipment. That means there was a magnetic disturbance, and paranormal investigators often link such happenings with the presence of a ghost. In addition, one of the team members started to feel ill while standing there.

As of 2008, the building was set for a renovation, Longshaw said. That includes the possible reuse of the uppermost floor as offices. It is mainly used as a storage area now.

And Tillman isn't the only haunted place on campus. The alumni office has a laundry list of spooks that it talks about on tours. Some students have reported seeing "handmaidens" walking around the amphitheater. It is believed these young women in very long prom-like dresses were members of a sixteen-person court that took part in May Day ceremonies in 1925. Then there is the story that the voice of Mai Rutledge, wife of President Johnson, can be heard calling his name. The voice is said to come from the Little Chapel, which was the school's first classroom. It is said that she calls his name when he leaves the space to wander campus.

Where does Johnson go? Besides back to work at Tillman Hall, he is said to have been seen inside Margaret Nance Hall, which is named after his mother. Johnson lived inside the building for a short time and maybe likes to visit it once in a while. Another ghost attached to the dormitory is of a student named Sandra, who wanders the halls looking for her room.

Then there is Crawford Health Center, which dates back to 1896 as the school's infirmary. It is named for Dr. Thomas Crawford, a well-known physician and one of the original board members at Winthrop. Students who have spent time in the infirmary have sometimes told stories about getting treatment from a handsome, elderly doctor with a square chin and glasses who says nothing to them. That matches Crawford's physical description. He just looks them over, then disappears.

Other students tell of seeing what appears to be a very hyper young woman carrying a suitcase or sitting on top of a steamer trunk in and around Lee Wicker Hall. The ghost is believed to be that of Lee Wicker, an English professor and wife of the college's second president, James P. Kinard. Wicker, according to the school's history, loved to travel. She loved to travel so much she would often pack up her steamer trunk and set off on adventure without telling a soul. People would only know where she had vanished to when she sent a telegram back to her husband from somewhere else. Students also report door knobs rattling when no one else is around. Maybe she is trying to find a new adventure?

Then there are the stories of men in military uniform walking around Bancroft Hall. It is possible these are the ghosts of airmen who lived in the building during World War II. Many of them went off to the war as pilots, never to return. And many of them left behind young brides and girlfriends among the Winthrop campus student body. Are they looking for their lost loves that they left behind some sixty years ago, or perhaps trying to find the last place they found peace before the war? Students and professors working late at night have been startled to hear mysterious footsteps marching in cadence up and down the hallways. Others have said they have seen doors slam shut when there was no wind and felt strange breezes flutter through a classroom when no window was open.

No matter what is happening, Winthrop seems to have a lot of ghosts. So, the next time you set foot on the Winthrop University campus, look quick. The person walking next to you may not really be there.

# Just Uncle Lloyd Walking By
## Spartanburg County Has Ghosts Galore

Spartanburg is the second biggest county in the Upstate, and it has a very interesting history, to say the least. It is one of only a handful of places to have two *Time* "Man of the Year" recipients, James F. Byrnes and William Westmoreland. It helped create the name Pink Floyd and the drumming foundation of the band Lynyrd Skynyrd. It was also the birthplace of the 1970s southern rockers the Marshall Tucker Band. The downtown was a thriving railroad town, while the northern parts of the county were summer vacation spots for many people from South Carolina's Lowcountry. But most important to this story is the number of ghost tales and haunts that are connected to Spartanburg. In another chapter, I focus on downtown haunts. This chapter focuses on those haunted houses and areas that are scattered around the rest of the county, ranging from an old farmer to a Revolutionary War soldier still on patrol in the western part of the county to the ghost of a firemen that can predict the call of a blaze in the southern part.

Debra Johnson shared one such story about her childhood home in Boiling Springs and a ghost dubbed Uncle Lloyd, who roamed the property for years. Johnson noticed early on that there was something not quite right about the home after they moved into it in 1957. Things would go missing, and then show up again two days later. The family would hear footsteps coming from the upstairs while they were in the basement.

Johnson's mother said that one night she thought her husband had gotten home late from work because she felt someone crawl under the covers. She turned over to say goodnight to her husband, only to discover there was no one in bed with her. However, she could feel the presence of someone on the bed and began pushing at it to get it out of there.

Years later, Johnson herself was in the downstairs when she saw a man walk by the window in the sloping yard. The man was wearing coveralls and an old, black farmer's hat. She expected someone to come walking through the back door at any second. But no one came. She went out into the yard, and no one was there. Other people would also see the old farmer, whom they soon dubbed Uncle Lloyd because that was the name of the family that had owned the land the house had been built on.

"It was always strange little things like that," Johnson said about growing up inside the home.

Of course, not all ghost stories are true. Some can be explained, sort of. One such tall tale involves the alleged phantoms inside the main theater auditorium at USC Upstate, which is the sprawling, ever-growing college campus just north of the city limits. Several people told me strange tales of lights flickering on and off during shows. Jim Cox, the theater program's longtime director, said there is a nonsupernatural (but still unexplained) reason for the phantom lights. The building's wiring was notoriously faulty and lights would flicker and turn on by themselves. Lights would turn on even when there was no power running to them.

"It was just a bit unusual," he said. "We could never figure it out."

In 2005, the building was rewired and the oddities in the light system ceased, Cox said.

"If there was a ghost, I am in the dark about it, which I guess would be a good place to be," he said. "However, I can see how the phantom lights could lead to a ghost story because so many people saw it happen during shows."

But all that with no power? Still sounds like a ghost.

Mike Roper, who does ghost tours downtown during the Halloween season, also has collected some good stories from around the county. One of them comes from the west side of Spartanburg County, along Nazareth Church Road, which is located off of Reidville Road. The story goes that a Patriot soldier on patrol along this road during the Revolutionary War was shot by his own men by accident. People have reported seeing a man wearing a tri-cornered hat roaming the Nazareth Church Road over the years. Could it be the soldier still on his final patrol? The road is historic in nature. A marker at the corner of Reidville and Nazareth Church states that the nearby Nazareth Presbyterian Church has been a key component of Spartanburg life since it was formed in 1766. The narrow two-lane road is lined with trees and old cemeteries, and would be the perfect place for someone to expect to see a ghost while driving along on a dark, moonless night.

One final haunted spot I found probably took the most courage I could muster. I drove down Highway 256 until I got to the Croft Fire Station, near the South Carolina School for the Deaf and Blind. I wasn't scared because of the story, but because I was about to go unannounced to ask some firefighters about ghosts. I was expecting them to laugh me out of the building, but as soon I said what I was doing, they said, "You're looking for Red." Was Red the person who could tell me about the ghost? No, Red was the ghost.

Assistant Fire Chief Jason Merchant told me that in the early 1990s a firefighter with another Spartanburg department was sent to battle a blaze at a textile plant. His job was to mount the massive ladder that jutted off of an engine and hung precariously over the blaze. The firefighter, who was nicknamed Red, mounted the ladder with skill and precision. However, the ladder collapsed and the fireman fell to the ground. Grievously injured, he was rushed to a hospital, but fell into a coma and died roughly eight months later.

His fire department took the damaged ladder truck out of commission and sold it to Croft, which is located just outside the massive Croft State Park, Merchant said. Croft outfitted it to be used as a service truck and had the ladder removed.

"And apparently we kind of brought Red with us," he said.

Merchant was hired in 1998, and almost immediately was told about the ghost that haunted the building. The odd things—doors slamming, walking sounds when no one else was there, and a water fountain that ran by itself—hadn't occurred before the department bought the truck. The Croft team began saying it was Red who was roaming the two-story, concrete structure. Merchant didn't believe the stories and figured it was a joke. That is, until one day when he was watching television in the station's day room. The room is almost a hub for the first floor. It has doors that lead into the service bays for the trucks. Merchant thought he was the only person on the floor at the time when he noticed a figure walk by one of the doors' legal pad-sized windows. He got up to investigate, but there was no sign of anyone else on the floor. A few weeks later, he and one of the captains were on the second floor doing some paperwork. It was around midnight, and they heard doors slamming downstairs. All of the doors are locked at night, but knowing the ghost stories, neither was inclined to go see what was going on. When they eventually did go down (after the slamming had stopped) none of the doors were out of place.

Red has made himself known in other ways as well. Merchant said he heard what sounded like a tennis ball banging on the walls one time. People have heard noises from the truck that Red died on that no one can explain. And finally, they have heard noises from the attic area, as if someone was collecting equipment to go battle a blaze. Amazingly, the Croft firefighters have learned that whenever they hear the attic noises, minutes later they will get a call about an actual fire in the territory. Apparently, Red still wants to fight a fire.

Merchant said the oddities happen enough that all of the veteran firefighters have gotten used to them. They tell all new recruits about what happens, but they usually are skeptical like Merchant was. It doesn't take long, though, for them to see and experience Red. The fire department has since sold the old fire truck, but Red has stayed on. And Merchant is no longer a full-fledged skeptic.

"You hear a lot of stories, but I don't believe something until I see it," Merchant said. He's seen Red.

# Haunted Tales from Upstate Cemeteries
## Maybe the Dead Don't Find Rest After All

There is something about a cemetery that raises the hairs on the back of one's neck. Just walking near one is too much for some people, and they will cross to the other side of the street just to stay far enough away. And many South Carolina cemeteries, with their moss-covered tombs and rows and rows of granite markers, are no exceptions—especially at night. However, most paranormal investigators and ghost hunters say cemeteries aren't the best places to look for spirits. The people there have been buried and remembered lovingly. Ghosts, according to theory, mostly haunt places where they have unfinished business. A burial is normally pretty final. Still, there are a lot of cemeteries in the Upstate, and some investigators say they are just as haunted as anywhere else, and have checked them to find out for sure. They have found ghosts preaching, playing, and simply wanting to be left alone.

Angel Johnson and the Rock Hill Ghost Hunters group have investigated numerous alleged hauntings in the Rock Hill area. One of their more interesting finds was in Laurel Woods Cemetery, located in the city's downtown. The sprawling city-block-wide cemetery is exceptionally well maintained and surrounded by an ornate black iron fence. Johnson said the cemetery dates back to the 1700s, which would put its founding close to those of the first settlements in York County. There were no stories attached to the cemetery. Johnson investigated the site simply on a hunch.

"I've found that the best stories aren't always known or widespread," she said. "Sometimes, you have to look for them. We try a lot of cemeteries because there is a strong chance of activity. If it's a creepy kind of scary place, we'll go."

So on a fairly sunny day, they ventured into the cemetery with video and audio recorders to see what they could find. Johnson would periodically call out, asking if anyone was there, and if so, what was their name. When they later checked the tapes, they heard the name "Scott" answering one of her calls. They decided to go back and see if they could find Scott's grave. Johnson decided to bring along her kids so they could see the old graves and learn a little about their town's history. She soon found a grave that she believes may be Scott's. It was of a Confederate soldier and avowed member of the Ku Klux Klan, according to the words etched into the stone, she recalled. She had again brought an audio recorder, and again she played it when she got home. As she listened, she could hear the sounds of her children laughing and talking. Then she heard an unknown voice ask, "Do you want to play?"

"That was the last time I brought my kids there," she said. "I said, 'Never again.'"

Voices weren't the only thing Johnson and her team found at Laurel Woods. Their photos picked up various orbs and unexplained mists. In one photo, what appears to be a child-sized apparition stands next to a tree in an area of the cemetery where there are numerous children's graves. Johnson later went to the spot and found a grave next to the tree. The child buried in the spot was named "Stephen." She asked out loud several times if there was anyone there. When she played her recording back, she picked up a voice stating "Hey" and "I'm Stephen."

Another cemetery she and her group have investigated is in the McConnells area. It is called Bethesda. Pictures taken there show a bluish swirl enveloping her. Johnson also said her group witnessed strange shadows in the cemetery. It would seem like

32

someone had walked by, but no one was there when they turned to look. Johnson said ghost hunters' eyes sometimes play tricks on them, but there were too many of these shadows to discredit them easily.

A final cemetery tale from the Rock Hill Ghost Hunters is from the Gregory Graveyard near Lancaster. It is a run-down and semi-deserted little patch of trees, shrubs, and old tombstones. Their audio equipment picked up the muffled voice of what sounded like a preacher giving a sermon and some children talking. The noises were there, but the words could not be understood. This could be the leftover voices from any number of burials at the tiny, decades-old cemetery. That may have been one of the best encounters the group has had, but Johnson said there is still so much more to explore in the world of the paranormal.

"We keep doing this because we keep wanting to capture a full-on body of a ghost with real features and the ghost talking," she said. "Some people think we're crazy, but that's what motivates us. Some people say if they saw that, they would run. Not me. I would keep going toward it."

Of course, York County doesn't have a monopoly on haunted graveyards.

An abandoned children's graveyard off of Poinsett Highway, near Furman University in Greenville, is said to have several nocturnal spirits. According to legend, people have heard the laughter of children emanating from the graveyard. The cemetery is very dilapidated and hidden behind a large apartment complex. The only access is by parking your car near Furman and walking an abandoned road to the cemetery. The tiny headstones peak out of the ground, and in some places the graves have collapsed, leaving the graves perilously exposed. Dry leaves and pine needles cover much of the cemetery where trees grow among the burial plots. Tiny iron fences gate off some of the plots, which seem to be scattered around the densely wooded area, as opposed to the straight rows that people have come to expect in graveyards. And while the legend states this was a children's cemetery, I found several graves that were dug for adults. It is definitely a very spooky little graveyard (probably less than fifty headstones), but really nothing out of the ordinary. And the only sound I heard was the noise of cars and trucks blasting by on Poinsett Highway.

The South Carolina Paranormal Research and Investigations group did an excursion into the cemetery next to Fairview Presbyterian Church in Greenville, said Shelley Armstrong, one of the group's investigators. The group was asking questions out loud and recording them, with the hope of finding some ghostly answers. The tapes recorded a woman's voice answering, "I don't know" and "It can't be" when someone asked if the year was 1864 or 1984. The cemetery's oldest grave marker dates back to 1797, and the church itself was formed in 1785 by three brothers, their cousin, and a friend, who got the land in lieu of payment for fighting in the American Revolution. According to SCPRAI's findings, more than forty Confederate soldiers are buried in the cemetery, along with numerous Revolutionary War veterans.

The current church dates back to 1858 and has been placed on the National Register of Historic Places. According to SCPRAI, several members investigated the property in the fall of 2007 and had some interesting finds. One woman with the group said she was walking by a headstone and got the sensation that someone had grabbed her. She felt dizzy and was breathless after the incident. Another member reported seeing a shadow pass by one of the graves when no one living was walking by and no animals were near enough to cast a shadow. The same member also felt an unnatural cold spot near a grave of a man who died in 1876. The headstone carried the strange epitaph that he left no living relatives. Several pictures taken in the cemetery, which is surrounded by a small stone wall, featured "orbs" in them when later developed. Unfortunately, the group reported an unusual amount of traffic on the road that day. The road is generally pretty quiet when it comes to vehicular traffic, and the extra noise caused problems in trying to record ghostly sounds.

A story from lower Greenville County involves Michael Chapman, who told me he took some pictures inside the Fountain Inn Cemetery that showed several strange orbs and ectoplasmic debris floating around. As he walked around the graveyard, he also turned on a tape recorder to see if he could pick up any strange noises. As he and his wife, Helen, went among the headstones, they noticed the grave of a young woman. Pictures of the woman were attached to the marble marker, and Helen Chapman remarked how pretty the girl was. When they later played back the tape, a woman's voice could be heard saying, "Who, me?" after Helen Chapman made her statement.

Another interesting ghost story comes from the Williamston cemetery. The story goes that an unexplained light can be sometimes seen darting among the stone markers. When people get close to the light, it vanishes and no one living is there. Could it be something reflecting off a piece of metal or nearby windows? The people I've talked to said that is not likely because the lights move as if someone is walking very solemnly among the graves. No one is quite sure who the possible ghost might be in this town located on the eastern edge of Anderson County. I have been told that the best time to look for this ghost, who is located near Williamston's historic downtown, is sometime between midnight and 1 a.m. and that the light can usually be spotted on the far end of the graveyard.

On the southwestern edge of Anderson County is the even littler town of Iva. There, a man can be seen walking inside the cemetery around dusk. When people get close, he is said to vanish right before their eyes.

Ed Bolt, the director of Hagood Mill in Pickens County, passed on a story about Illinois Baptist Church in Pickens. The story goes that the cemetery, which is located off of Highway 135 just before the Pickens city limits, is home to the spirit of a little girl who died in the 1800s. The cemetery is very old, with numerous fading headstones that date back several hundred years. There are even the graves of slaves inside the cemetery. At least three people over the years have told him that a person can take a tape recorder into the middle of the cemetery and press the record button. They won't hear anything while they are there, but when they play back the tape a feeble, but angry voice of a young girl can be heard saying, "Go away, go away." Bolt said he has never tested the story himself. One other note is that unlike the spirits in many other ghost stories, this one is said to be most active when the sun is shining.

"It's odd, because every time I had just about forgotten the story, someone will always bring it up," he said.

Just off Highway 20 in Abbeville County, there is the Long Cane Cemetery. Heidi Brumbelow of the Georgia-based Heritage Paranormal Society visited the cemetery located on a hill one chill autumn night. They took numerous pictures and video in the graveyard, which dates back to the mid-1700s, but didn't think there was anything there. Brumbelow said she hadn't heard of any particular ghost stories, but wanted to try it because of its age. However, when they got home and reviewed the tapes, they noticed what appeared to be the apparition of a balding man wearing a blazer strolling by in one of the pictures. They had not seen anyone living walk by while they had been in the cemetery that night.

A cemetery with a history of strange spooks can be found in Spartanburg, adjacent to Converse College. Students at the all-women's college (which is known for its fair share of ghost stories) nicknamed the old Oakwood Cemetery's gothic entrance "the gates to hell" or "Hell's gate" because it is so eerie and sinister. One story goes that people can't get cell phone service while standing among the graves. The place does have a somewhat scary feeling to it, but the supernatural's ability to control cell phone coverage must be worse than my own cell provider's, because I had no trouble making calls while visiting the site. Mike Roper, who does ghost tours in the city of Spartanburg, said that is not the only story. Many people have claimed to see and hear mysterious children playing in the cemetery. More people have taken pictures that contain orbs and odd mist inside the very large cemetery. It is built on somewhat of a bluff overlooking the Converse campus on one side and railroad tracks on the other. During one of Roper's 2007 ghost tours, one man was snapping pictures out the side of the trolley while it was stopped in the cemetery. He called Roper the next day to tell him about something very eerie that had come up on one of the shots. There through the window, the face of a child could be seen staring back into the trolley. Needless to say, there were no living children near the trolley when it had been stopped at Oakwood.

"It is one of the clearest photos I have ever seen," Roper said.

Cris Crissinger was the person who took the photo. He said he didn't notice the face on his viewfinder that night, and didn't discover it until he looked at it the next day on his computer.

"I was absolutely astounded by it," he said.

Crissinger said at first he suspected it may have been some kind of a hoax, so he examined the dozens of other photos he and his wife took while in the cemetery. There was nothing else at all. A skeptic, Crissinger said he had never experienced anything paranormal before that picture. The photo later got posted on the Internet, but they took it down because it created a sensation as hundreds commented and debated about its authenticity.

Roper said other people have told him about a tall woman dressed in black with dark hair who can be seen wandering the graveyard tapping on the tombstones with a walking stick. Some people have reported feeling a stick hit them while they have been in the cemetery by themselves. Could this ghostly woman be telling them to get out of the way? City police officers periodically have found evidence of Satanic markings in the cemetery, but Roper could not say how much of that is real and how much is just pranks played by people trying to create scares about an already creepy cemetery. Other police officers have reported strange, unexplained noises while parked in their squad cars near the cemetery at night, Roper said.

Now, Roper is a skeptic about ghosts. He does the tours more out of his deep knowledge of local history from his years as an investigator with the city fire department than for the love of a good scare. Yet, he can't quite explain what happened to him one time at Oakwood. He will often let people walk around the cemetery to take pictures while he uses a wireless microphone to tell them some of the stories. One time, he was walking and he felt like someone came up behind him and shoved him. Roper stumbled, but was able to turn around quickly to see who his assailant might have been. No one was there. When he got back to the trolley, the driver asked him what had happened. The man had seen Roper stumble and wondered if he had twisted an ankle.

"I said, 'You wouldn't believe me if I told you,'" Roper recalled.

# The Red-Haired Man
## A Ghostly Story from Old Pendleton

It's hard to believe, but the little town of Pendleton in Anderson County was once the largest metropolis in the Upstate. Of course, that was more than two hundred years ago, before the various counties such as Anderson, Oconee, and Pickens were formed, and Pendleton really wasn't that big in the first place. But after all of these years, a great ghost story can still be told about this little town.

It revolves around the Hunter Store, which was the town's main mercantile goods shop after opening in the 1850s. Named after the family that ran the business, it was vacated in 1929 when a larger store was built next door. It stayed that way until the 1960s, when the Pendleton Historic Commission started renovating the building to become the tourism board's new headquarters and gift center, said Jo McConnell, a longtime employee with the commission.

Employees worked long hours getting the building updated, she said. Plumbing had to be added and electricity had to be run to the two-story wooden structure in the heart of Pendleton. One night, the agency's director, Harley Batters, called his wife to tell her he needed to work late and to not fix him dinner. He said goodbye to the staff, locked the doors, and went upstairs to get some work done. It wasn't long, though, before he heard what sounded like something fall to the ground downstairs. He went down the wooden steps and peered around the rooms. Nothing was out of place, but then he heard what sounded like someone walking around on the second flood. He didn't bother to investigate this time. He just called his wife and said he would be home soon.

It wasn't that much longer before one of the descendants of the store's owners came by to see how the renovation was going. Batters said things were going well, but relayed the story about the mysterious footsteps and noises. The man, "Punch" Hunter, said he could tell him who was walking around. It was the ghost of the man who had died in one of the upstairs rooms in the late 1800s. A friend of the Hunter family had been riding his horse near Eighteen Mile Creek, which runs less than a mile from the store. The man had imbibed a little too much alcohol and fell from his horse into the creek. Someone found him and brought his limp body to the store because it was the closest building that had a spare room. The man seemed fine enough— just a little wet and tired—when they pulled up to the building. They hauled him up to the caretaker's room on the second floor so he could sleep off the effects of his drinking. It was a spring evening, and they just left him in his water-soaked clothes and extinguished the lamps. But an unexpected cold snap rolled through the region that night, leaving a bitter frost on the spring trees and flowers. Anyone in the Upstate knows this kind of late frost that sends a person scurrying for extra blankets and woolen socks for their feet. The young man didn't get that opportunity. When the store opened in the morning, he was found dead in the upstairs bedroom.

Hunter's story unnerved the staff. During the renovations, they had found numerous things written on the walls in the upstairs rooms. There were things such as measurements and little notes about events and weather readings. One was in the caretaker's room. Written on the wall next to the door were the words, "cold, very cold, May 19, 1894." The staff had thought it was interesting and had framed it as kind of an almanac of what was happening in Pendleton so many years before. They were now wondering if that might be a clue as to the day the young man died. McConnell said they are not sure if it was written in memory of the man, or possibly as a last scribble to let people know he died that frigid night.

Soon, staff started to notice more odd things happenings. They would be on one floor and hear something fall on the second. It would be followed by the sounds of someone running or scurrying away. They never found a trace of anyone up there. Then the ghost decided to make his presence better known, McConnell said.

One of the women was working downstairs and heard what sounded like creaking footsteps pacing along the upper floor. She thought nothing of it even though there was no one upstairs at the time. Everyone at the commission had gotten used to the ghostly noises by that time. But then the steps started heading toward the staircase. The woman looked up because this was new. The sound of feet slowing hitting each step soon followed. The woman peeked around the corner to see what might be coming down. She was hoping there had been someone upstairs. The shape of a man in a dark, crumpled suit came into view as the sun shone through the back door. The man stopped on a little landing at the base of the stairwell just before three more steps jutted in an L-shaped direction. The man's head was covered by thick, curly red hair that matched the beard on his face. He stood there for a second and simply vanished. No further walking down the steps. No saying anything. No going out the back door. She did nothing, but later told her co-worker.

The ghost wasn't done making his appearances. McConnell would be the next person to see him. She left the office to get a drink from the water fountain. One of the other employees heard McConnell, and later said McConnell made the strangest sound she had ever heard. When the woman looked up, McConnell was clinging to a nearby countertop. The woman rushed to her. Was she sick? No, McConnell answered. She had just spotted the curly haired man. McConnell said when she rounded the corner, she spotted the silhouette of a man crouched down between the bookshelves. He was a large man,

41

and he appeared to be hunching over as if he was hiding from someone. McConnell said he was nothing more than a dark shadow, but he definitely appeared to have curly hair, just like the last time the ghost had been spotted. The image lasted only a few seconds, but scared her very much.

Later, two more people confirmed the sightings, McConnell said. She was speaking to a Leadership Pendleton class about the history of the region, and especially the store and the commission office. She mentioned the ghost story at the end of the presentation just to see how people would react. Afterward, two teachers in the class came up to her. They had seen similar things while working in the building as teenagers. They had never told anyone about it because they didn't want people to think they were crazy. The staff also believes that Batters's grandson may have seen something in the store one time. The small child was playing in the store after closing hours while the staff worked elsewhere in the building. All of a sudden, he came back into the offices to ask who the man inside the building was. Everyone rushed into the main area to see what was going on. No one should have been there, and when they got to the room no was around. There were no signs of anyone outside the building either. They asked the child what had happened, and the child answered, "He's gone."

"We don't know what happened that time," McConnell said. "Was it a child's imagination or something else?"

As the years have passed, staff members at the Pendleton Historic Commission have come to appreciate their ghostly denizen. Actually, when I called the office to ask about the ghost, McConnell cheerfully answered you mean "our resident ghost." They believe they know his name, but don't reveal it out of respect for his family's descendants, who still live in the area. The big thing they have always talked about is trying to track down a photo of the man from when he was living to see if he had red, curly hair, McConnell said.

And they also wonder about what to do with the penciled-in note in the caretaker's bedroom that states "cold, very cold."

The letters have faded over time, and McConnell said they have talked about ways to preserve the note. It is a remnant of the past that no one wants to see lost.

"I think it verifies our ghost," she said.

# Silent Footsteps
## Scary Stories from an Old Hospital

Pam Schliffka grew up enjoying ghost stories—especially true ones. Something about the aspects of an actual haunting sparked her interest. As an adult she made yearly trips to some of the more haunted towns and places along the East Coast. Little did she know that she likely could have canceled her trips when she took a job at an assisted living facility for the elderly in Greenville. The building she worked at was haunted by any number of spooks and specters that cried out in the night, rode the elevators, played the harp, and even left footprints along a wet floor in what was once an operating room.

The facility was located in a former hospital. The original structure is a rather large building, but today looks nothing like what one would expect of a modern hospital. Its brick facade and southern-style white columns give it a very Southern gothic look. It looks more like an antebellum mansion that you see in old Greenville photographs than anything else. And maybe—just maybe—the switch to being an assisted living facility is what has sparked the paranormal activity. Paranormal activity is often associated with construction or unwanted changes.

However, Schliffka didn't know any of this when she started there in 1995 as an activities coordinator for the patients. Actually, the first few months were fairly routine, with no hint of what might happen in the next few years. One day, however, one of the facility's administrators relayed a chilling tale. She had been in an office and saw as plain as day a series of footprints in a slick of mud and water along the floor. The prints started midway through the room and ended a few steps later. There was no way anyone could have walked there without her seeing or hearing them. And the fact that the footprints started and stopped midway through the mud bothered her.

That story led to some of the staff telling about things they had seen, Schliffka said. And they would continue telling the stories as more and more people saw things. There was a phantom child seen in the dining room every so often. Then there was a young woman in there as well, but she did not seem to be connected to the child. Some people reported hearing children's voices when no kids were in the facility. Others said they had heard the sound of a baby crying at odd hours.

Then several staff members reported seeing a very tall man wearing a hat and scarf waiting for the elevator. He would stand there until the bell gave its familiar ding and the doors opened, then pace forward and vanish.

Schliffka said most of the events happened in the late afternoon or early evening—unlike most ghost sightings, which seem to occur at night.

The staff started to do some investigating into the building's history. Countless patients had spent time there over the years nursing themselves back to health. Some died. Could some of the strange goings on be related to that? They also found the story of a young man, just over twenty-one, who volunteered at the hospital in the 1950s. While working in the operating room, he accidentally turned on the laughing gas and died from the accumulating fumes. Gail Boudreau, the woman who saw the footprints in the same room years later, said it was very chilling and associated the death with the footprints.

"There was no way someone could have walked back there," she said.

Boudreau also told a tale of how she and another employee were filling out timecards in the late afternoon when they saw the shadow of a man walk by the door. They went into the hall-way to see who may have been there at that time of the day. No one was there, but they could clearly see a man's shadow pacing along the tile floors before it vanished into the dark corners. That scared them, and soon more people would see the mysterious man. The building alarm was activated one night around 1 a.m., and Boudreau and other staff rushed to the building to see what might have happened. They could find no reason for the alarm, but took time to make some sandwiches for the startled residents. That was when they saw the indistinct outline of a man walking down the staircase. They could only see his hat and head, and figured he was one of the security guards even though they weren't supposed to be there at the time. But then one of the administrators came in and asked the staff why they were all gathered around the stairs. They said they were trying to figure out who had just walked down. The administrator said it was definitely not a security guard because none had been called out that night.

"Just then, we heard the door shut," Boudreau said.

Next came a story from one of the cooks, who said she was preparing meals in the kitchen when she noticed a woman with very long gloves and a veil over her face sitting in the corner. She looked real, but the cook was bothered by the strange clothing. The cook knew all of the residents and staff there, but didn't recognize this woman. She turned the other way to ask the other cook if there was a new resident. The other cook said no. Both women turned around to look back in the corner. The veiled woman was no longer there. The whole event took less than a few seconds.

Several staff members had worked in the building when it was a hospital, and they said there had been some unexplained things over the years, but that the events had definitely escalated after it became an assisted living facility. Maybe some of the spirits there got restless when the building changed its purpose?

"It was spooky," Boudreau said. "But I wouldn't say it was scary. At least not all of the time."

One of the scary times was when Boudreau was washing her hands in the ladies' room. She heard what sounded like very beautiful harp music coming from the hallway, followed by the sound of young children crying. Boudreau rushed out to the hall to see what was going on. The noises stopped the moment she left the bathroom, and no one was in the hall. She asked a co-worker if someone had been playing something on a radio or a CD player. Nothing.

As for Schliffka, the job was a mixed blessing. She was a big believer in paranormal activity and ghosts, yet she never saw, heard, or experienced anything. It was kind of like being a kid in a candy store who isn't allowed to get any chocolate, but Schliffka said it was still a neat experience.

A few years after she left, a new group bought the facility and changed its name. She knew the new administrator and gave him some advice about the possible ghosts and haunts.

"He just kind of raised his eyebrows," she recalled.

# Haunted Houses Across the Upstate
## Some Scary Stories That Would
## Frighten Any Homeowner

Shelley Armstrong remembers when she learned—or at least consciously realized—that her childhood home in Sharon was haunted. She was fifteen. She and a friend were hanging out in the living room talking to another friend on the phone when they simultaneously noticed a glass on a bar across the room start to move. Her friend calmly got up, walked outside, and said she would never spend another minute in Armstrong's house ever again.

"And she didn't. Whenever we did anything from that time on out, it was at her house," Armstrong said. "And it was a pain, because it was a long drive to her house."

More of a pain than living in a haunted house?

"No, that was normal for me," she said.

The ghost came to be known as Herman for no other reason than because Armstrong's mother felt the ghost needed a name that wouldn't frighten everyone. Herman was mostly kind to Armstrong's family, but he had had some problems with the previous owners, she said. An elderly couple had lived in the large, rambling, two-story house before them, and had completely boarded off the home's upstairs. The reason was that the man had once felt a hand grab his ankle and try to throw him down while he was walking down the steps. The couple left all of their furnishings on the second floor and never went up there again.

Armstrong's family moved into the house when she was around nine, and she said she never really noticed anything, but added that there were probably things that happened and she was too little to remember them. They didn't even know about the incident on the steps since the realtors had reopened the second floor before showing the house to potential owners.

The normalcy all started to change after the moving glass incident. After school, she would go to the back door to let herself in. The door was always locked, but one day she got home and the door was unlocked. Nervous, she crept into the house and grabbed one of her father's rifles. She proceeded to go room-to-room, calling out that if anyone was there, she had a gun and would use it. (The gun, by the way, was not loaded.) She went upstairs and checked the rooms. No one seemed to be there. Maybe her parents had forgotten to lock the door that morning for some reason. However, when she got to her room, all of her clothes has been taken out of the drawers and piled on the bed. This bothered her, but she didn't think it was a ghost. Maybe a prank by her brother? He denied it when he got home, and she sort of shrugged it off. The next day, though, it happened again. Unlocked door. No one in the house. Pile of clothes. And it kept happening for about a month. Each time, she would put her clothes back and wonder what was going on. Finally, she was walking out of her room after another cleaning and had just taken a few tired steps down the staircase when she heard a noise from her room. She rushed back and found all the clothes out again. Herman had struck in a matter of seconds.

Herman would create other kinds of disturbances as well. Keys would get moved or go missing. Strange voices could be heard when no one else was around. It got to the point that if her brother was upstairs and making noise, he would holler down that it was him, and not Herman. Armstrong moved out when she was eighteen, but moved back in with her husband a few years later to help take care of the home. One night they were in bed when they heard what sounded like a cinder block crashing in the attic. She went upstairs to check, but there was nothing there except insulation. Her husband was exceptionally creeped out by living in the house, which dated back to 1780, but couldn't explain why. He would go visit her when she was working third shift because he didn't like being there alone. The couple moved out in less than six months. To this day, people around the little town of Sharon know the house's reputation for being haunted, she said.

However, Armstrong remains keenly interested in hauntings and the supernatural. In 2007, she helped form South Carolina Paranormal Research and Investigations. The group has chapters in the Lowcountry, Midlands, and Upstate, and its goal is to investigate as many hauntings as possible. One of the first was a private residence in Anderson where the owner complained of numerous unexplained things that happened while he was sleeping. Strange noises could be heard and lights turned on and off for no reason.

Joey Armstrong, one of the investigators, joined the team as it set up in the little home. The house had been built in the quiet Anderson neighborhood in 1951, and one of the owners had died in 1975. His widow died in 2004. A new family purchased the home in 2007, but noticed some odd things, which is why they contacted SCPRAI. The family told the group that a baby gate at the top of the steps often slammed by itself and that they heard footsteps tramping up and down the steps when they were trying to sleep.

The team went about taking basic temperature readings and testing for electrical currents. The idea is that dramatic spikes in such readings could be a sign of paranormal activity. The group also uses divining rods, which are two metal wires attached to a pair of hand-sized wooden knobs. These, too, are supposed to help find unexplained phenomena. The group was ready for some big stuff based on the information they had gotten from the homeowner. But the night proved to be somewhat inconclusive. The ghost or ghosts were not making much noise. A psychic with the group said she felt a presence in one room. The woman said she saw a shadow in the master bedroom, but the spirit was not willing to talk. Meanwhile, Armstrong got a strange reading in one of the children's rooms. One of the lightbulbs was still hot to the touch despite not having been on for more than an hour. Armstrong did a temperature reading and found it was at more than 80 degrees. Even after the homeowner went to bed, which was when the hauntings normally occurred, nothing major happened.

The pictures the team took later revealed orbs that acted in a strange manner. The orbs seemed to follow the team members from room to room. They snapped a picture of one orb in an area where a cold spot had been found. Other orbs appeared to be playing as they went down a hall. Armstrong said this was the first time they ever saw orbs behave that way. But the orbs went unseen at the site.

After a few more hours, the group decided to pack up their equipment and head home. The homeowner locked up the house and went to work. The team was standing outside talking about the night and hoping that some of their recordings had picked up things their ears had not. That is when they heard a door slam inside, and the sound of a little girl giggling. They ran to the front of the house, less than twenty feet away. Looking through the window, they could see that the removable baby gate had been put in its place at the top of the stairs even though no one was inside at the time.

"That was the ghost that messed with us," Armstrong said. "I have a sense of humor that won't quit, and this ghost was a jokester."

A. J. McJunkins, another team member, was working the recording equipment that night. He said he picked up a strange whirring noise inside the house, almost like that of a high-tension power line, which he has yet to be able to explain. But that is not the most interesting recording he has made in an Upstate house, he said. The group was doing another investigation in a house in Pickens County, off of Highway 86. He was asking questions aloud to see if anything would answer. For some reason, he was asking a lot of questions that would have been more suited for a man. Do you use tobacco? What brand? Etc. But for some reason, he got the feeling that he might not be looking for a male ghost, but maybe for a female one. He asked, "Are you a girl?" When he later played back the recording, the sound of a woman screaming could be heard after that question.

"I think she was trying to let us know she was there and wanted to talk, but didn't know how," he said.

Shelley Armstrong said it has been fun looking for ghosts across the Upstate, but there is one place she doesn't want to investigate. It's her former home in Sharon.

"I just want that to remain in the past and part of me," she said. "I don't think I really want know what may have been there."

Another Upstate haunted house belongs to Randy Berry of Newberry. Berry and his family moved into a Victorian raised cottage in the early 1980s and went about renovating it. The high-ceilinged house dated back to 1874, and little did they know it at the time, but there was a tragic story attached to the building. But first, here's how they found out about it. Berry slumped down into bed one night after a long day. His wife was already asleep, while his infant daughter was in her crib in the next room. His eyes had barely closed when he thought he heard a noise. As the cobwebs left his head, he could hear soft singing coming from the nursery. His daughter must have woken up, and his wife must be trying to quiet the child with some lullabies. A rational explanation until Berry realized his wife was sleeping soundly next to him. He sat straight up in bed and rushed down toward the other room. As soon as his hand reached the doorknob to the nursery, the singing ceased. His daughter was snug and asleep and there was no sign of anyone in the room. A few days later, he was talking to the elderly woman who lived across the street from him. He mentioned the singing in passing, and the woman didn't seem too surprised. She figured he had known his house was haunted. It was a well-known haunting around town, and that is why she had never mentioned it to him before.

Haunted? That can't be, he said.

According to the neighbor, a girl between the ages of eight and ten fell down the staircase shortly after her family moved into the home in 1874. She told him the girl had been buried in the backyard, but he has never been able to prove it. The woman gave him the phone number of a family who had lived in the house in the 1950s and had an experience with the little girl. Berry called the family and got a chilling tale. The family's mother was making beds one day when a little girl appeared in the room. The child didn't say anything, but started helping on the folds and tucks of the bed sheets. The mother asked the girl questions, but the child remained mute as to who she was and why she was inside the family's home. The mother and the little girl went room to room without the child saying anything, despite the woman's constantly telling her that her family must be worried about her. Finally, after all of the beds were made, the child simply vanished.

Perhaps the same little girl was still roaming the house, Berry thought. Another night he was in bed and heard something on the steps. It sounded like the gentle footfalls of a child going up the staircase. It was very even walking, so it couldn't have been his daughter, who was just learning to climb steps. He heard the feet get to the top of the stairs and then start back down. By the time he got out of bed and was at the top of the stairs, the noises had stopped. He checked the house. No one was there.

That was one of the last times, though, that the family had anything unexplainable happen to them. It's been more than twenty years, but he said it was never really a scary experience. They felt it was a friendly ghost who simply wanted to help them get accustomed to their new home.

"There were no spots of cold air or things flying across the room. It wasn't like the Amityville Horror or anything," he said.

And while many haunted houses have a tragic history attached to them, at least one that I found had somewhat of a happy ending. Cam Larson said her family passed down the story of their ancestral home in Simpsonville. Her great-great aunt owned it, and before she died she asked Larson's grandmother not to let the beautiful white, two-story home be destroyed. Larson's grandmother fought for more than a year to save the house from the wrecking ball and finally got it saved. The first night in the saved home, she and her husband had just gone to sleep when she felt something on her cheek. It felt like a very tender kiss—almost like it was in gratitude. She looked to see if her husband had kissed her. He was fast asleep. Larson's grandmother surmised that her aunt was paying her one last thank you for saving the house.

# The Horrors In and Around
# the Rock House
## Strange Things in Lower Greenwood

Steven Wooten is a skeptic when it comes to the supernatural. He looks for every possible answer when trying to deal with the unexplained, and many times he can find one. Yet, he had an experience at the famed Rock House in Greenwood that even he can't explain.

I use the word famed when describing the Rock House because there are so many legends attached to the two-story structure just south of the city limits that it is hard to even count them all. It has been the one place that generations of Emerald City residents have whispered and talked about. You probably had a similar place in your own hometown. It was the creepy abandoned building that housed any number of unknown horrors for those brave enough—or at least dared enough—to check out on dark, moonless nights when no one else was around and teens were looking for a little bit of a scare. The events that gave rise to the legends and ghost stories at the Rock House have become muddled over time. Everything from a house fire's killing an entire family, to a whole family's being murdered inside the dwelling, to a murder-suicide is said to have occurred on the very spooky piece of property. That has led to generations of people telling stories about strange noises and lights at the house. And despite numerous no trespassing signs located on the road leading to the building, the tales of the macabre bring an untold number of people to its abandoned door-step each year.

If there is anything true about the building, it is that it is very scary and dread inducing, even during daylight hours. The story goes that the house was built sometime in the early 1800s after several wooden structures built there burned to the ground. While that creepy history would have warned off most homebuilders, the owner decided to one-up nature and build a house made of stone and rock. (It should be noted that when I called the local history museum to get information on the building, the director said he had never heard of the structure or the stories.) The large boulders and rocks that make up the walls have greened over the years, and add to the general creepiness. Two chimneys poke out of where the roof used to be, and the large rectangular windows, long devoid of glass, give the structure the look of a sunken, mournful face with horns coming from its head. Four stone columns support what used to be the front porch. Graffiti covers most of the inside and outside of the walls. In what may have been a misguided attempt to scare people, someone tried to draw an upside-down star, which is often associated with Satanism, but the symbol ended up looking more like the Jewish Star of David affixed in a circle. A grand spiral staircase is said to have once graced the house, but it is long gone. Very heavy woods around the building add to the feeling of foreboding and dread.

That is what Wooten found the first time he and his friends went to the site to explore it and the stories attached to it. He said it was creepy, but he felt nothing out of the ordinary. Wooten went several other times, and being the skeptic that he is, he dismissed the stories associated with the building. There were no ghosts. It was just an old house that sparked silly stories. And when a local rock band asked him to take some promotional photographs for them there, he thought nothing of it. They wanted a creepy place, and he really didn't mind going back out there on a warm spring night. Driving out there, though, one thing was different. The band members joked around that they hoped something would happen. No one had said that when Wooten had gone out there with friends before.

The band and he parked their car down the road. The moon was high enough that they were able to use the light from their cell phones to guide their way past the blooming trees of early spring. As far as they could tell, they were the only living things out there. They entered the front door, and Wooten remembers seeing a small tin can lying in the room to his immediate left while the band looked for a place to pose for their photos. They were setting up when they heard the unmistakable clink-clank rattling of a kicked tin can. Wooten immediately remembered the tin can, and the group went to the front room. The can was on the other side of the room from where it had been before. They looked out the windows to see if anyone was outside or if a wind gust might have blown it. There was nothing outside and the air was quiet and still.

They returned to the other room and started snapping photos, then heard the tin can being battered around the room rather violently, as if someone was kicking it back and forth. Again, they hurried to the room and found the can lying on the other side of the room. It was the beginning of a series of odd events that they could not explain as they scoped out the house for places to shoot. As soon as the clanging can would die down, something else odd would happen. They began hearing someone running laps around the perimeter of the house at a very fast pace. They glanced out the windows, but saw nothing. Wooten had spent many hours in the woods growing up and had learned how to use lights to find the glowing eyes of an animal. He angled his cell phone to let its glow peer out into the wilderness. There was no sign of an animal. They started to discuss what might be happening. Was this someone's prank or something else? Maybe something supernatural? As they were talking, one of the band members found a seat on a window sill. All of a sudden, he flung backward and would have tumbled the three feet to the earth if the others in the group hadn't snatched him up. The man told them he felt someone grab the back of his T-shirt and pull him backward. Deciding to carry on conversations away from the windows, they formed a circle in the middle of one of the rooms to talk to each other. Wooten said they started to notice a freezing moisture start to form on their arms. It was almost like something was rubbing against them one or two at a time and leaving them cold.

"It was like nothing I had ever felt before," he said.

After about two hours of these off and on phenomena, they left the house and headed back to their car. They never saw any evidence of any other living persons out there. The next day, Wooten began looking at the photos on his computer screen. There were numerous bright lights floating around the band members. The lights shifted from picture to picture, which made Wooten believe that this was not the reflection of the flash off of a piece of metal or glass that may have been outside. Many paranormal observers describe these unexplained lights as "orbs." Wooten said he was able to get a close-up of the orbs, and they appeared to be almost three dimensional in shape as opposed to just flashes of light.

Wooten is somewhat at a loss as to what happened there that night. The only thing he can surmise is that the band members' desire to see and experience something may have spurred whatever paranormal entities reside on the grounds to make their presence known.

"It's hard to say what happened and why it happened," he said.

# Smoke from the Chair
## More Ghost Tales from Abbeville's Belmont Inn

Some people see ghosts. Some people hear them. Some people feel them. But it is not every day you can smell one. Yet, that is what happened to a group of Georgia-based paranormal investigators when they went to the Belmont Inn in Abbeville in 2007.

Bobby Bishop has investigated dozens and dozens of alleged ghosts, spooks, and haints in the mountains of northern Georgia and South Carolina. These hilly areas are filled with tales that are told to make a person's skin crawl, but Bishop has found that most of them are left wanting when it comes to actual reality. He believes only three of the sites he's investigated were truly haunted by something from the other side.

One of those is in the historic Belmont Inn, located on the town square in Abbeville. In *Ghosts of Upstate South Carolina,* I described Abbeville as one of the most haunted places in the entire Upstate and said it probably ranks with Charleston as having the most ghosts per capita of any place in the Palmetto State. There is a ghost chair in the opera house where a woman in turn-of-the-century clothing is said to watch performances from time to time. There is the tale of the Civil War–era ghost of a mysterious set of stairs in a bed and breakfast, and then there is the story of a chair that rocks on its own and never collects dust in a house on Main Street. The town has become somewhat of a popular ghost hunting attraction and even has a monthly ghost walk highlighting some of the more well-known stories. There is also a reenactment of one ghost story inside the beautiful Trinity Church, located just off the town square. Heidi Brumbelow said she set up a "Phantom Fest" in the town in 2007 because of its charm and ghostly lore.

"It's really not fair that so many people focus solely on Savannah or Charleston," said Brumbelow, president and founder of the Heritage Paranormal Society. "People would be crazy not to investigate this town."

The Belmont Inn is no exception to the ghost tales. With its grand antebellum wraparound porch and high brick veneer, the building looks like the perfect place for spooks. A ghost named Abraham as well as a spectral Scotsman are said to live on the staircase. Kitchen staff tell tales of knives and plates flying off the shelves. There is even a story of a phantom bellhop that made a wake-up call for a guest even though a power outage had knocked out the need for the call from the computer systems during the night.

It was these stories that led a large number of paranormal researchers from across the Southeast to head to the town a few weeks before Halloween 2007. Many of them set up times to investigate the various haunting at the various locales, and Bishop of the East Georgia Ghost hunters said it didn't take long for them to realize there was something going on at the Belmont besides happy guests enjoying a charming South Carolina town.

One couple saw the investigators running around with their cameras and sensors their first night there and asked the team what they were doing. Instead of being a little bothered by the fact that there were ghost hunters poking around where they were staying, the couple was intrigued because maybe this group could explain what had happened to them. They had heard voices just outside their room's door the night before. When they went out to check, no one was there. This happened several times through the night. They couldn't quite understand what was going on, but said it was too random to be pranksters. Would the ghost hunters mind checking their room?

"We almost did it to humor them," Bishop said. "I'm glad now that we went in."

The group set up an infrared video camera and started rolling. They stood behind the camera's view screen and watched the silent, oddly glowing green room, and were about to shut down and tell the couple that there was nothing in the room besides bed sheets and dressers when something happened. They saw a shadow pass in front of the camera. It was indistinct, but it was not a normal occurrence. There was no one in front of the camera, and no way to recreate the image unless someone walked directly in front of the lens. Or at least something, as they say in most horror movies. Was the darkened image of a ghost on the tape? A review of the footage confirmed that the shadow was there. Bishop quickly took the tape to a forensics expert, who said he couldn't explain what it was on the tape.

"I definitely feel we caught something big," Bishop said.

That was not the only thing his group found inside the historic 1903 hotel. He said there were at least twenty-seven different sites in the twenty-room building that contain some kind of unexplained activity. The hotel has a long and colorful history. City leaders led by a P. Rosenburg envisioned the idea of a grand, modern-style hotel in 1901 to help aide Abbeville's growth as a resort destination and a stopover spot for people travelling to Atlanta. They awarded a $25,000 contract to a Georgia firm to build the structure, and the Eureka Hotel opened in August 1903 to rave reviews about its beauty and grandeur. The Eureka thrived until the 1950s, but slowly went into decline as the interstate system took travelers away from Abbeville. The hotel closed in 1972, but was reopened and restored in the mid-1980s. A decade later, the Peterson family purchased the property and made more improvements. The Petersons know the ghost stories, but don't take them too seriously.

"I'm petty open to it," said Alan Peterson, one of the owners. "But I have to admit, I've never seen or heard anything."

Peterson said it was interesting to see the investigators going about, but it didn't really bother him.

"I don't have time to think about it," he said.

Peterson said he agreed to let the investigators come into his hotel because he wanted to see if they actually could find anything or if the stories were just the products of some overactive imaginations. In addition, he felt the event would be a good thing for Abbeville's downtown.

One employee told me that the ghost stories seemed to change with the waitstaff, but Bishop's finding show that maybe there is some truth to many of the well-travelled stories. And maybe there are things going on that no one quite realizes yet. While his findings didn't show actual proof of the phantom bellhop, his group did find proof that something was happening in one room that couldn't be explained. Several guests have claimed to have seen a man standing beside them who then almost immediately disappeared before they could wipe the sleep out of their eyes. Was this the bellhop, or another ghost? Heidi Brumbelow said her team also was at the Belmont and picked up a shadow crossing their camera's path in yet another room.

Another member of Bishop's group was riding the service elevator when he felt what seemed to be a hand tap him at the base of the neck. The man is a skeptic about the supernatural, but confessed to Bishop that it was the creepiest feeling he had ever experienced.

And then there was the smell of a ghost. There is a chair in the lobby area that is located near the main dining room. It is said that it was the favorite chair of a former town lawyer, and that he often smoked his pipe there. The man has been dead for years, but the smell of burning tobacco still wafts up every now and then. Bishop admits he was skeptical until he sat in the chair, which has been cleaned numerous times. The smell was there. Several members of his team took a seat, and they, too, reported the sensation of tobacco odors around them.

"It was unmistakable," he said. "This wasn't residue. This smelled like a freshly lit pipe."

# Some People Have No Luck
# When Buying a House
## Greenwood Family Lived in Two Haunted Houses

Their neighbor thought Joyce and Mark Maxson were lucky as anything, but most people would have thought differently if they had known the truth. The Maxsons, though, take the whole thing in stride. The story dates back to more than twenty years ago, when they lived in a little neighborhood in the city of Greenwood. They had gone on vacation for a week, and when they returned they got a somewhat envious message from one of their neighbors.

"She said, 'That was so nice of your grandmother to come by your house every day,'" Mark Maxson recalled.

The only problem was that no one was supposed to be in the house while they were out of town. And since nothing was missing from their home, it didn't make any sense for a burglar to come in and do the dishes. They could reach only one other conclusion. It was a ghost. That may sound irrational, but for the Maxsons it made sense. But it was a rather tame experience compared to all that would happen in their next home.

That house was first constructed in 1830 as a log cabin and underwent a massive expansion in 1906 to its current Victorian-style splendor. Somewhere along the way, someone added some ghosts. The Maxsons have seen a man walking up and down the halls as well as in the garden area. There is the ghost of a woman on the second floor who likes to play little gags.

And then there is a little boy. The few times he has appeared, he has seemed more frightened to see them than they were of him. Oddest of all, the Maxsons actually learned the names and lives of some of the ghosts. Maxson said seeing or experiencing the ghosts is not an everyday thing, but it has happened enough during their twenty-plus years in the home for them to become really interested in the paranormal.

The first ghost they saw was a man wearing a white outfit wandering the hallways. The vision never lasts long before he would vanishes. However, it is long enough to get a good look at his face and see he is an elderly gentleman. The ghost later began making appearances outside, but there he wears a dark outfit while strolling among the trees and gardens. The second ghost is definitely that of a female spirit. She likes to play tricks, especially on the family's daughter. It is nothing malicious— just silly things like moving a pencil around the room or hiding little objects when a person's back is turned. Doors open and close for no legitimate reason. There have been the jingling sounds of sleigh bells. Their old Irish Setter used to enjoy chasing a softball-sized blue light through the house, and sometimes vice versa. One time, the light flew through the dog's four outstretched legs. Maxson's lasting memory of that event is of the Setter with its head tucked down and looking backward to figure out what had happened.

A third ghost, though, may be the most interesting. The couple was watching television one night when they saw a very real-looking young boy wearing blue jeans and a peach-colored shirt come running around the corner of the room. The boy was lost in his own little world of childhood play. But he skidded to a halt when he saw the Maxsons. His mouth dropped and his eyes opened wide. Mark Maxson said it looked as if the boy had seen a ghost.

"It probably was the same way I was looking at him," Maxson said.

The entire event lasted just a few seconds, then the boy simply disappeared.

The boy has made only one more appearance to the family, but it was a monumental one. The family pulled their car up into the driveway and was unloading some things. Their daughter went inside first, through the side porch, and the family heard a blood-curdling scream come from inside. The concerned parents ran inside to see what was the matter. Their daughter was standing in the kitchen trembling. She told them she had walked in the door and had seen the head of a little boy floating across a countertop before it vanished as if descending into the floor. It likely was the same little boy Maxson had seen near the television, based on the description his daughter gave. But why was only the head seen? Maxson learned that at one time a set of stairs led through where the kitchen is now located and that the steps went to the house's back door.

Some paranormal researchers theorize that time and space overlap ever so slightly. They think that this overlap may explain some supposed hauntings and ghosts. To the spirit, there are still stairs leading down through the kitchen as opposed to the present countertop.

While the little boy remains a mystery, Maxson has learned the identities of two of the other ghosts in the building. Joyce and Mark were telling their story to a friend at a party one time when someone asked them where the house was located. They told the woman, who said she had lived in the same house as a child and probably could help them with their questions. She brought them some old photo albums and asked them to see if they recognized anyone in the very old black-and-whites. They quickly found the man they had seen in the hallways and in the garden. His last name was Jones, and he had lived in the house for years. The woman could also explain why he changed clothes. The man was a farmer, and always wore dark clothes when working outside. However, Jones also dabbled in real estate and sold many prominent homes around Greenwood over the years. Guess what his suit color of choice was when selling. Correct. He wore white. The Maxsons' daughter recognized one of the other ghosts, the one who always liked to play tricks on her. She was Miss Ann, a former school teacher who had lived in the house.

"It's kind of fun to know who our ghosts are and have pictures of them," Maxson said.

The hauntings are not an epidemic, he said. They have happened enough over the years for the family to know that they are not alone, but not enough that they are a constant nuisance. Maxson said they get real active every once in a while and then go dormant. One of the most recent was during a party around Christmas 2007. Their daughter had placed a drink on a counter, and it started making noises. Maxson quickly grabbed a camera and snapped some shots. The resulting photo showed mysterious white orbs between his daughter and the cup.

"It just shows you they are always ready to make themselves known," he said.

# Three Voices, Many Ghosts
## Some Interesting Finds in Chester

It doesn't take long to find a ghost story in Chester. Pretty much everyone in this rustic and quaint little burg has some story about ghosts that haunt the former Chester Little Theatre, which is the two-story building with a classic marquee right out front on Main Street Chester. The tales are numerous and plenty and bring droves of paranormal experts and ghost hunters to the little town, all trying to find what if anything still haunts the building. And for one group of ghost hunters, they found enough at this haunted locale to say there are at least three legitimate ghosts if not more inside. The Palmetto Paranormal Research Group has recorded at least three different voices during their several investigations of the building. Two appeared to be tied to two of the more famous hauntings, but the third voice may be the most interesting of them all.

The building itself has a very unique history in Chester, which is located in the bottom corner of the Upstate. No major interstates run anywhere near Chester, which helps create the feeling that the town really hasn't changed in generations. Many of the buildings in the little downtown can trace their heritage back for generations. The old Little Theatre is no different. The structure was built in the 1920s as part of the local telephone company's operation and has a large basement. That is where the first ghost story emanates from, like the heat coming out of the local swamps in late summer.

The story goes that in the early 1930s a fire broke out in the building after a boiler exploded in the basement. People rushed in panic as black smoke filled the rooms, but one man came to the front in an effort to restore order. It was the son of the company's owner, and he bravely led people out of the horror and onto the streets outside the building. But the young man went back inside to look for others, thinking that somebody else might still be trapped inside. He never got back out. The second major story attached to the building is that of a young woman who was brutally assaulted and killed in the alley that runs behind the building. Many people say the ghosts of the young woman and the brave man still roam the building to this day.

It was these tales that first grabbed the attention of Michelle Mayes, president of the Palmetto Paranormal Research Group. Her group started in 2003, and this was one of the first stops on their journey of trying to uncover where there are and where there aren't haunts.

However, Mayes and her team soon learned that there were more than just these two ghost stories attached to the building. Many other occurrences had happened there that couldn't be explained. There are the tales told by people who have worked on plays there over the years. Stage crews told Mayes they would sometimes hear the soft sound of children crying coming from inside their headsets during shows. There was no earthly explanation. Another story goes that the crew used a tape recording of a tune gleefully entitled "The Death Song" for one show. The song ran properly the night of the first show as a piece of background music during a key scene. The crew members left it overnight, and when they returned in the morning, they rewound the tape to play again that night. Luckily, they checked it first. The song had somehow re-recorded itself playing backwards in the few hours they had been away.

"The stories had floated around for years," she said. "It's a huge spot for paranormal activity."

Mayes said she was pretty excited to be exploring the building the first time she went there. She was the first of her group

69

to enter, and admits she was a little nervous as she walked through the large glass doors. She has been interesting in the paranormal ever since childhood, and these were her first footsteps into a truly haunted place.

"I'm not one get to spooked, but I could feel there was something lingering there," she said. "That really was interesting."

One of the members of her team was a skeptic, and even he started to get a strange feeling as he walked around the building. There was a feeling of fear so intense that the hairs on his forearms stood on end. Something was definitely in the air as the theater's director guided the group to the grand balcony, up and down narrow flights of stairs, and to the hardwoods of the stage stretching across one side of the building. The building was ripe for a ghost hunt.

The team set up its equipment—infrared cameras, audio recorders, magnetic detectors, and the like—in hopes of capturing something. Many paranormalists use these kinds of equipment to scientifically track spirits. And yes, these researchers were ready to find some good scares. Mayes decided to see what the ghosts might be up to. She called out to see if anyone was there. When they played back the audio equipment at a later time, a voice could be heard clearly stating, "Yes, I'm in the back." Mayes believes it was the voice of an unnamed stagehand who wanted to be an actor but never quite made it. Legend has it that the man stayed around the theater for most of his living life, and now was doing the same thing in the afterlife. He was simply looking for some long-lost recognition for his work in the theater, she surmised.

"I would say he is a residual spirit," she said. "He is somewhat quiet and stays near the stage area."

That was not the only EVP (a term used to describe a sound that is not picked up normally by human ears) that they found when they played back their recordings. One was of a man's voice saying "hot." Mayes is convinced it was the voice of the man killed in the fire. He is still trying to tell people about that horrible day. Another voice was a woman's crying and sobbing

70

words unintelligibly. The group is convinced they recorded the lingering voice of the murder victim.

Mayes said she also had some strange feelings while walking around the building. Going down a set of narrow stairs, she felt very uneasy and sick to her stomach. She later learned that a woman had been thrown down those stairs after an assault in the 1950s. A picture taken of Mayes shortly after that uneasy feeling shows strange colors and shapes around her. Mayes said it was a vortex that was enveloping her.

They also saw what appeared to be a man pacing the balcony with his hands in his pockets. The man appeared to be irritated that they were snooping around inside the building. When the group played back the recordings of the event, they heard a voice state "coming down the stairs." They were unable, though, to get any pictures of that ghost—he vanished before they could get a shot.

Mayes's was one of the last paranormal groups to investigate the building before it was sold, and the new ownership doesn't like people messing around there, she said. The theater group moved to a building across town, and to date they haven't had any ghost troubles. Or at least ones they are talking about publicly. So be warned before you go looking for the ghosts of old Chester Little Theatre. The current theater with the words "Chester Little Theatre" on its marquee isn't the one you are looking for, and the one you want to see doesn't want to see you.

# Stories from the Very Haunted Town of Pickens
## Sarah McDaniel Has Some Company

If you've lived in the Upstate for any amount of time, you've probably heard the story of Sarah McDaniel, the resident ghost at the Pickens County Museum. Located just a few blocks from the town's Main Street, the museum was once the county jail. The wife of the first county sheriff to live in the building while it was a jail, McDaniel was a doting mother to her thirteen children, but she died after an illness in 1903. The story goes that her ghost stayed behind to take care of her beloved home and children and that her presence can sometimes been seen in the upstairs room where she died.

But there may be more than just one ghost in the two-story building. While two additions to the building were added over the years to serve as exhibit and lecture space, unsurprisingly the majority of the various hauntings are attached to the old jailhouse part of the structure. Several past and current workers, talking on the condition that their names not be revealed, told me several hair-raising stories revolving around an old piano, a Confederate's soldiers frock coat, a worker who was scared to be left alone, and odd noises from a ramp leading into the gift shop. The employees do not think that Sarah McDaniel is responsible for all of the odd and scary things that happen there. However, the museum isn't the only place that is alleged to be haunted downtown.

The offices of the *Pickens County Courier* are located on Garvin Street, about a block off Main, in a single-story white house that was once a doctor's office. Actually, two separate doctors used the building as their home before a series of newspapers took over the building starting in 1990, said Rocky Nimmons, the *Courier*'s publisher. Nimmons was one of the first people to experience the ghost. He was working late one night putting the final touches on the paper. It was around 1 a.m., and he heard what sounded like a crash come from a back room. He got up to check out what had happened, but found nothing out of place. Nimmons said this was a very loud crash, as if a whole set of shelves had come tumbling down all at once, and he was perplexed. The noises recurred every so often for the next few weeks, and several staffers told Nimmons they had experienced other odd noises.

One day, Nimmons was working in a camera room and he got a strange thought in his head. Now, it wasn't an outward voice talking to him, but for some reason he could hear the voice of a little girl stating, "Algernon, Algernon." Nimmons asked some of the staff if they knew what the word meant. Despite some guesses, no one was quite sure. Actually, no one had a clue until a worker picked up a dictionary and looked up the word. One of its meanings is "one with the mustache." Everyone wondered what that could mean, but Nimmons developed a theory. One of the doctors who used to live in the building was a very well-known man around town named Reinovsky. The respected doctor had been known to pace the sidelines at Pickens Blue Flame football games, and his most recognizable physical trait was a white handlebar mustache. Could the whispering child stating "Algernon" be looking for Reinovsky. Now, Nimmons is quick to note that this is likely an odd coincidence, and there is no proof that whatever could be haunting the building is connected to Reinovsky. In reality, the ghost has become somewhat of a catchall for anything that cannot be explained. If there is a problem, someone will almost always blame "the doctor."

"It's a lot of fun," he said. "This is not a scary ghost by any means."

However, there is one odd twist to the story. Many of the employees at the *Courier* were former staffers at the *Pickens Sentinel,* which was housed in the building until October 2006, when it moved to a new building up the street. When they formed the *Courier* in the summer of 2007, it was somewhat of a logical choice to move back into their old digs. The crashing noises were not heard for months, and some staffers wondered if the spirit had moved on. Just two days before I went to interview Nimmons, they heard the unexplained crashing noise in the middle of the night.

"It was that booming sound again," Nimmons said. "This building has a lot of history to it."

Just a few blocks away from the *Courier*'s office is the museum, which still looks very much like a nineteenth-century jail, with its castle-like turret facing Pendleton Street.

Allen Coleman, the museum's director, said he could not verify how many of the building's ghost stories were true, but said a lot of people do ask questions about them. The staff have discussed bringing in professional ghost hunters and paranormalists to investigate the strange goings-on.

"Then we could know once and for all," he said.

The first story is of a beautiful piano located in the basement of the building. The piano had once belonged to the McDaniel family. The staff came in one morning to find three of the keys had been torn off. The damage wasn't bad and they were able to reattach them. However, the piano's keys continued to come off at an alarming rate. The last time it happened, the keys were left on the stool. That led one frustrated employee to say out loud that the ghost should stop trying to destroy the antique piano and that the staff were simply trying to save it for future generations. The piano problems stopped, but that didn't stop many more odd things from happening.

Another employee confessed to hearing what sounded like footsteps heading down the ramp into the gift shop area. It was her first Saturday working in the museum by herself, and she didn't know what to think. Maybe the ramp was always making noises from settling or pipes underneath and she had never noticed them when there were other people around talking and walking around the building. Still, she kept looking out to see if someone had entered, but no one was there. Later on during the day, she heard what sounded like hushed whispers from that area. Again she went to look, only to find no one nearby. When another staff member came in, she asked if there were ever any strange things that happened in the building. She had expected her fellow employee to think she was crazy, but the other woman simply said there were a lot of unexplained things that happened at the museum. Another employee said she saw a large clock come off the wall once and fly across the room.

"It was very spooky to know that, but it didn't bother me after a while," the woman said.

Then there was the "busy corner." No matter what exhibits were put in that room, something would always go wrong, several staff members said. The most interesting example involved a Confederate soldier's frock coat that was hung over the shoulders of a mannequin. The coat would be draped normally when they left at night, but on the ground when they came in the next morning. At first they thought that it might not have been placed on the mannequin correctly. Or that a large truck had passed by during the night and that the vibrations had shaken the coat to the ground. However, they soon noticed that the coat would fall in odd ways (such as with the arms spread out or the next time tucked) and be found in spots where it simply couldn't have dropped to by itself. One worker said that one time he actually felt someone punch him square in the chest when he went to pick up the coat. It was hard enough to startle him, but not enough to knock him over. The museum is not sure who the coat belonged to during the Civil War, but apparently the former owner doesn't want someone else wearing his coat when the South rises again. Or maybe the ghost is a Yankee.

75

The punched worker was not the only person who made contact with a ghost. One woman said she constantly felt like someone was walking behind her as she made her way around the museum one weekend. Another employee later refused to work in the building by herself because of all of the ghosts hanging around.

So, maybe the next time you are in Pickens, say hello to the doctor and Sarah, but keep your coat to yourself.

# Hub City Haunts
## Scary Stories Abound in Downtown Spartanburg

For generations, children growing up in the neighborhoods surrounding the old Spartan Mill site knew better than to dawdle when the sunlight started to fade over the smokestacks on the west side of town. If they waited too long in the night air, the story went, Booger Jim might come down the railroad tracks and snatch them before they made it home for supper.

Booger Jim was the ghost of a man beheaded one night decades before by a passing locomotive, and his restless spirit still walked the rail line near the Spartan Mill. But as children grew, they discounted the tales of Booger Jim as superstition and stories told by their mothers to get them home on time.

At least until Mike Roper came along. Roper is the host of a Halloween time Spartanburg ghost tour, and he has painstakingly researched some of the scary tales that surround the Hub City's downtown area.

"I've scanned microfilm until I didn't know it was any more humanly possible," he said.

Roper, a lieutenant with the city fire department, said the story behind Booger Jim is based in fact, and is one of the many corrupted ghost tales of downtown that has a spark of truth somewhere in its past. In September 1931, a railroad worker was killed at the Arch Street intersection along the main line that runs through Spartanburg, which was dubbed the Hub City because of the amount of rail activity that once hummed through this Southern town. The man did lose his head.

As for the story of the man's still haunting the line, well, Roper, isn't so certain. But people have told that a strange bluish light can be seen roaming the rail line at night near Arch Street, which is about two-tenths of a mile away from the Magnolia Street train depot. That is where Roper starts his tour, which has become a popular Halloween season attraction. His trolleys are regularly filled with people looking for ghosts.

Roper got the idea of a ghost tour as a result of his job, which requires him to inspect downtown buildings for fire safety. Over time, he learned stories about possible haunts and unexplained things happening inside the various buildings. He also knew much of the non-ghost-related history as well. Being a skeptic, he has spent hours trying to find stories that can be backed up with historical evidence, such as the true story of a man being struck by a train near Arch Street.

The tour fits nicely into the revitalized downtown Spartanburg. It wasn't that long ago that downtown was a proverbial ghost town at night, but private and public investment have helped turn the district into one of the jewels of the Upstate. Now the ghost tour helps brings people downtown. In 2006, a friend of Roper's who runs the downtown trolley asked him if he could help put together a one-hour tour. Roper now jokes that he has collected enough information to run a four-hour tour.

"I really feared that I wouldn't find enough haunted places," he said. "I was definitely wrong about that."

After the train depot, the group makes it way to Morgan Square, which is filled with ghost stories. Morgan Square has been the heart of Spartanburg since the early days of the twentieth century, and while the area's fortunes have ebbed and flowed, the ghost stories have been steady. One of the major ones involves the current location of the Extended Stay America building. In 1977, a former structure on the site known as the Andrews Building was scheduled for demolition. Built in 1912, it was the first "skyscraper" constructed in Spartanburg. However, the multi-story building caved in on itself before the demolition could occur. Five construction workers were killed in the collapse as brick and steel tumbled down toward the street. The incident was the most deadly single accident in downtown Spartanburg's history. For most of the next twenty years, people would report seeing construction workers walking the grassy lot at odd hours of the night where the Andrews Building had been located. People would shine their lights on the workers to see who was there, and they would vanish. The sightings ended when the new building was constructed.

Another site on Morgan Square is the old First National Bank building, located at the corner of Dunbar and Magnolia. The legend often told is that a man was crushed when the vault was being put in place, and that his ghost haunts the building to this day. Roper found the real story.

"I would say that is the most haunted place in Spartanburg," he said.

In 1942, the bank managers hired a man named Otis Brock to move some heavy safety deposit boxes into the basement storage area. Brock, who ran a moving company, decided the best way to do the job was to place the box system on a rope and pulley and guide it down the steps on a plank that was being used as a slide. Brock got on the back end of the boxes to guide them down. As they inched close to the bottom of the stairs, the rope broke and the metal units came tumbling down on him. His men jumped down the stairwell to save him while other men ran out to the street to frantically wave down help. Brock was unconscious at the bottom of the stairs—but not dead. He would die three days later at Spartanburg General Hospital.

The legend goes that Otis Brock's ghost is still in the basement trying to warn people about the dangers on the stairs.

Former bank managers said female employees refused to go down in the basement for years unless they were in groups because of the eerie presence.

The building later was converted into restaurant space, but that has not stopped Brock from trying to warn people. One of them was Roper, who visited the building while researching its history. Now Roper is a skeptic. He thinks much of the unexplained can be explained.

"People like to be frightened," he said. "I think a lot of people so want to believe that they will take anything they can't quite explain and say it is something more."

Yet, when he was down in the basement, he felt like something grabbed and then tugged his shirt. Being a skeptic, he passed it off as nothing major, but just a little odd. However, when he was telling a friend about his research in the building, he mentioned that he had experienced something odd in the basement. The friend asked simply if he had been grabbed by something unseen, and Roper said yes. The friend said that happens to a lot of men down there and that maybe Brock is reaching for help to this day.

Bernie Kavo, owner of Justin's Steak House, said he heard about the tales of doors opening and closing and other strange events when he moved his upscale restaurant into the building in 2007. To date, nothing out of the ordinary has happened to him or his staff. While he is familiar with the true story of Brock's death, he wonders how much of it has been played up over the years.

"We kept waiting for the air conditioner to break down or something like that," he said. "But we've never had anything out of the ordinary happen. Maybe the ghost is just resting. Or maybe he likes us."

One more Morgan Square ghost is said to be located in the Wild Wing Cafe at the corner of Main and Church streets. The building was once home to a department store in the 1930s and 1940s, and the legend goes that a young man hanged himself on the second floor. Roper is quick to point out that he can

80

find no record of a death, which tends to make him put some doubt to the story. Staff at the popular bar and restaurant have reported odd things on the second floor, such as footsteps when no one else was on the floor. Others have reported items going missing, only to show up moments later exactly where they were supposed to be.

Thomas Hawkins, the Wild Wing Cafe's manager, doesn't give much credit to the tale. They started when a customer, who claimed to have psychic powers, told them she sensed the presence of the young man who had killed himself. After that, every unexplained thing that happened on the second floor or on the stairwells was chalked up to being supernatural. He had one assistant manager who always seemed to be hearing or seeing something ghostly. Hawkins, himself, has never seen anything out of the ordinary.

"I don't believe it," he said. "There are a lot of old buildings downtown and it is easy to start stuff about them."

A little bit away from Morgan Square is the Evans Building, which used to be the home of Spartanburg High and is now a general use building for city and county offices. The large building is one of the landmarks downtown, and even after all of these years it looks like an urban high school, with its large windows, ornate entranceways, and faded brick facade. The ghost story goes that players are still battling out a basketball game from a bygone era inside the second-floor gymnasium. The squeaky sounds of sneakers on hardwood, the echo of balls dribbling, and the huffing of people running up and down the court can be heard.

The large room is now used to house voting equipment most of the year. So many people have claimed to hear the noises over the years that it is almost a fact of life for many Spartanburg residents. Current employees, though, said they really couldn't say how much of it was true and what has been made up over time.

Of course, Spartanburg's two downtown colleges have plenty of spooks, which I chronicled in *Ghosts of Upstate*

*South Carolina.* At Wofford College, there are stories of strange noises at the Carlisle-Wallace House, which was used as a rehabilitation building for Confederate soldiers during the Civil War. At Converse College, the former head of the music department, Hazel B. Abbott, is said to haunt the auditorium that bears her name. Then there are stories of a Mary G., a former dorm mother who still looks after the students inside Pell Hall.

Dozens of additional stories seem to be created by students each year. Two former Converse students, Lauren Blakeley and Natalie Chapman, told me that there are still a lot of things happening on the campus. Both reported seeing closet doors open all by themselves while they were students in the mid-2000s. They also heard doors violently slam shut in rooms where all the doors were wide open.

Another student from the early 1990s told me about one encounter. She was going to bed one night in her bunk bed at Pell Hall when she thought her roommate said good night from below. So, she said good night back, which caused her roommate to ask why she had just said good night twice in a row. The student explained that she thought the roommate had said good night first. The roommate figured it had been her.

All three Converse College students I spoke with admit that there seem to be a lot more stories than would be expected at the scenic downtown women's college. Roper agreed to some extent.

"There are probably more ghost stories than students at Converse," Roper said.

One more ghost story from downtown Spartanburg involves Roper and the train depot. He came back from doing his tours one night and approached his truck to drive home. He always makes sure to lock the doors before leaving and he has the only key, but as he approached he noticed something very odd. The seats were slid back and folded up into the cab of the truck. However, the doors were locked. Roper quickly checked the truck. Nothing was missing, and there was no sign of any damage.

Had Booger Jim paid him a visit?

"I can't explain that one," he said. "Why would someone break into my truck just to move the seats around."

# A Ghost Named Earl
## And More Scary Stories from Abbeville County

Located off the edge of Abbeville's quaint town square is a three-story, white wooden building. A somewhat rather pleasant building during the day, it takes on a much different identity at night. That is because the third floor of the more than 150-year-old structure is haunted by the ghost of an African American man violently killed there at the turn of century. People have reported seeing a face in the upstairs windows at night— peering out for help that likely will never come. And at least one paranormal group that investigated the building found a lot more. A broken camera, strange lights, and a psychic who had to be carried from the building in fear were among some of the incidents.

May Hutchinson, Abbeville's resident grand dame of spooky stories, filled me in on the history of the building. It was built in the 1850s to serve as the county jail. The building was a classic example of Southern architecture. It was designed in the Robert Mills style and constructed by the state public works commission. (Mills, one of South Carolina's most famed architects, lived in Abbeville during the 1800s, thus the choice for the building's design.) For years, prisoners with mental problems were chained to the floor to prevent them from hurting themselves and others. Despite being of antebellum construction, the building served as the county jail well into the 1970s before a new, more modern facility was constructed. The building later served as the county museum before being shut down due to safety concerns. The county is currently trying to restore the building.

However, for most of the last century a ghostly tale has revolved around the building, and it started with a man named Earl Miller. According to a medium who visited the structure and later told Hutchinson about her findings, Miller was a twenty-eight-year-old black man who was lynched on the third floor after a dispute over money in the early 1900s. Newspaper records confirmed the death. Since then, the building has become a popular curiosity spot for people looking to find a ghost. A slight chill seems to surround the building, and its dark windows add to the feeling of dread inside. If there was place for a ghost to hang out, this would be it.

This was one of the many ghost stories that drew a large contingent of ghost hunters and paranormalists to Abbeville in the fall of 2007. Mark Maxson of Greenwood drove over to see what all the commotion was about. He has had numerous experiences with the supernatural. At the time, he was thinking of forming his own ghost hunting team in Greenwood and was hoping to get some pointers. Instead, he joined the Heritage Paranormal Society after a very interesting weekend. Their first stop, of course, was the old jail and the search for Miller's ghost.

"The jail was really awesome," he said.

He joined a small group of people who entered the building at around 11:30 at night. The autumn chill was already thick as they walked through the ornate wood-and-glass doors. They took temperature readings and scanned for electromagnetic fields. The idea was to create a baseline for what was happening in the building. Temperature and magnetic fluxes are often linked with paranormal experiences. The group quickly made its way up the winding stairwell to the third floor, which is where most of the ghost stories are centered around. They began snapping pictures.

Flashes lit the room and the sound of digital cameras being checked filled the air. Maxson said he heard one of the young women gasp as if shocked. Everyone turned to look at her. She said that she was taking her photos when it felt like someone grabbed the camera and tried to wrench it from her hands. She went to check the photos stored in the memory and noticed that the lens had been cracked. The woman showed the others her camera, and someone saw what appeared to be a fresh fingerprint across the lens when no one living had touched it. Could the ghost have been a little camera shy? Heidi Brumbelow, Heritage's founder and president, said a technician told them the damage could only have happened from the inside. Maxson said there was definitely an odd feeling there, like the presence of someone unseen was hanging over the room.

Shortly afterward, a psychic who was with the group suddenly collapsed to the ground in tears. The woman said she was experiencing the pain of Miller's last moments as the mob descended on him in a frenzied madness. Brumbelow said the woman began to also wail that it felt as if somebody was trying to take a baby from her. The woman had to be carried from the building.

While this was going on, several of the ghost hunters found images of "orbs" in their pictures. Maxson is not a big believer in orbs' being a sign that something supernatural is always present, but he said a lot of people were getting them on their camera screens.

After about an hour inside the building, the group decided they had seen enough and headed out. They locked the doors and made their way into the grassy, tree-lined courtyard. The Heritage Paranormal team always ends an investigation with a prayer to make sure that anything inside the building stays there and does not follow any of the members. Maxson said he looked up during the prayer and noticed a face looking out at him from one of the upstairs windows. At first he was not sure what he was observing. It could have been an optical illusion or the way the glass was made, so he asked his daughter to look at the window when the prayer was done.

She looked up and said she saw a face. Several of the other people present also saw the face looking forlornly out of the glass panes. They asked the team leader if anyone else was inside and if the doors were locked. He confirmed that they were all out and that the doors were locked, but as the group edged along the side of the building, the face stayed in the window sadly looking down on them. Oddly, Maxson said it looked like the face of a Caucasian rather than that of an African American. They could see the face looking at them until they got to the street.

Their next stop was the Burt-Stark Mansion, which is located on the other end of downtown in a neighborhood populated by classic Southern-style homes with large, sweeping porches and gothic columns supporting the roofs. The Burt-Stark Mansion can easily be called the last stand of the Confederacy. This is where Jefferson Davis held his last official war meeting, on May 2, 1865, before the Confederacy's hierarchy split up to evade the pursuing Federal forces. It has been said this was the place that Davis decided to end the fighting. It proved to be a fitting coda for the Rebel cause. It was Abbeville County that had first voted to secede from the United States four years before. And it created a ghost legend. Jefferson Davis is said to be one of the many specters haunting the building.

The Greek-revival home was constructed in the 1830s, and remained in the Stark family until the last member of the family sold the structure to the Abbeville County Historic Preservation Commission. Unlike the former jail, which oozes creepiness, the Burt-Stark Mansion is the exact opposite. It has been fixed up to its antebellum beauty and features numerous period artifacts and furnishings. There are even some Confederate flags in the rooms.

Madelyn Ashcraft is on the board of the Abbeville Historic Preservation Commission, and she also serves as a docent for the tours of the beautiful structure. She has spent many, many hours inside the building and has been there late at night. She can say unequivocally that she has never seen or heard anything unusual inside the mansion. Now, there are some creaks and groans every once in a while, but she attributes that more to the structure's age than anything supernatural. However, she will not go so far as to say that she is a skeptic.

"I've never seen a whale up close, but I have seen them on television," she said. "That's how I feel about ghosts to some extent."

Still, Ashcraft and the rest of the historic society's board decided to let the group of ghost hunters into the building during the Halloween season because they believed it was in the best interest of Abbeville. The town has made a name for itself in the last few years as a very haunted little place to visit. One of the historic society's core goals is to promote the history of the quiet little county, so they decided to open the mansion to investigators.

Ashcraft was one of the people present when the Heritage Paranormal team set up shop during the fall of 2007. She admits she still didn't see or hear anything when they were there, but the team members said there was definitely something interesting going on at the historic site.

"You never know what will happen until you try it," she said.

Heidi Brumbelow noted with some pride that hers was the first group ever to investigate the historic structure.

"It was definitely one of the most haunted places I have ever been in," she said.

Maxson said they split up into four teams upon entering the building. Each team would investigate one part of the property, then proceed to the next section without telling the other teams what they had seen. The idea was to see if the ghosts were appearing to more than one group. It also served as a safeguard against anyone trying to embellish a story told by one of the other groups.

Maxson was one of the first people to experience something definite. He was part of a group exploring the second floor. In particular, they were investigating a back bedroom where Davis is alleged to have slept during his one night in Abbeville. Several of the people there said they felt the presence of a man in the room. While this was happening, Maxson went into the hallway and saw the clear outline of a woman descending the steps. She was wearing period clothing, and definitely wasn't part of any of the ghost teams. His sighting was later confirmed by one of the teams that had set up the ghost hunting equipment on the first floor. There had been a magnetic flux and a drop in temperature on the steps around the same time that Maxson had seen the woman.

"It was interesting that they were able to pick her up on the stairs," he said. "The EMF readings went sky high."

The next place that Maxson and the rest of his group went was a separate outbuilding that had been used as a kitchen at one time. Some of the pictures they took showed a large grouping of orbs around a spot on the ground behind the building. Remember, Maxson doesn't put a lot of significance on orbs, but these ones would grow to intrigue him.

One of the psychics later said she picked up the presence of two African Americans in the kitchen. One of the women was very talkative and trying to talk to the medium. The other seemed to be very upset by that fact. The medium learned that one of the women's babies had died, and had been buried behind the building. The spirits showed the medium the spot. It was the exact location where Maxson's group photographed the orbs.

One final encounter in the kitchen building may have been the most surreal of them all. There were two rooms in the building, and two people in the group felt someone tap on their foot while they were standing in front of the fireplace. It was almost like someone had taken a soft step on their toes. And while the feeling was a tap, the sound was like someone banging,

89

and it could be heard from the other room. After that, Maxson decided to join Heritage Paranormal. And once again, when it comes to finding ghosts, it is hard to top the stories that surround Abbeville.

"It's just a spooky little town," he said.

# The Pretties and the Monster
## A Story from Greenville's West End

No one likes moving. There is the hassle of packing everything into boxes, the tossing out of things you don't need, the transporting all of the things you own, the unpacking everything at the end and finding new places for it all. Yeah, moving isn't fun. But it can be much worse when that process stirs up dormant ghosts and spirits. That is what happened to one West End business owner several years ago. There were spirits that became known as "the pretties," an imp that liked to kick the back of people's knees, unexplained flickering of lights, and a ghost who seemed to be stuck in a perpetual loop.

Beth Jones (not her real name) opened her studio in 2000, and quickly made a name for herself with her unique handmade art. The business grew over the next few years, which led her to look for a bigger space in 2005. Luckily, she found a new home for her business right across the hall from the spot she rented in a building on Main Street. Unluckily, that is when the haunting began.

She started noticing some odd things in the hallway during the move. First there was what appeared to be a woman dressed in clothes from the late 1800s. She would just appear and disappear at random. Then there was a ghost that Jones soon nicknamed the Running Man. She or her assistant would be at the main register and see out of the corner of their eye a man in a dark overcoat whisk by the open doors at a rapid pace.

By the time she or her assistant could steady their vision, the man would seemingly vanish into a brick wall. Then there was a blur of what Jones described as almost an energy field in the shape of a man. He would come into the studio at a normal pace, and then reverse his steps at a high speed, almost as if someone had hit the reverse button on a DVD player. While both women were noticing the odd things at separate times, neither of them said anything. They couldn't explain to themselves what they were seeing, and wouldn't know how to explain it to a co-worker.

That would change after Jones installed a series of silver halogen lights on the walls inside the studio. The lights came out of the wall on slim metallic arms and would be used to illuminate jewelry on glass shelves. That night, though, Jones woke up at 3 a.m. with a terrifying thought. For some reason, she got the strange feeling that her store had flooded and that her assistant was going to turn on the lights without looking inside. The combination of water and electricity would kill her. Bothered by the vision, she rushed to the store early that morning to get there before her co-worker. The vision proved to be prophetic. Water was all over the floor, but somebody else had taken care of the electricity. All of the lamps had been torn out of the wall and placed on the shelves, all in the same position. The walls still show the damage from where the lamps were torn out.

There was no way that the dozen or so lamps could have ended up in the same position without someone placing them that way. Jones knew she hadn't done it, and at the time there were only two keys to the store. She had one, and her assistant had the other. When her co-worker arrived a few minutes later and asked what had happened, Jones quickly crossed that person off the list of possible overnight handymen, which left her with the thought that it may have been ghosts.

"That made me think they were trying to protect us," she said of the ghost removing the lights before the water fried the circuits.

That is when they decided to compare notes. Both of them had seen the woman in the hall, and the Running Man. They both had seen the energy blur so frequently that they had gotten used to it, and were actually surprised when a real person entered.

But the oddities would continue. The computers never seemed to work right. They crashed frequently. The halogen lights would flicker and dim. Anyone who has ever been around halogen lights knows that is not normal. In the fall, they would smell the distinct odor of burning wood. Jones remembered a story about the former Chicora Women's College having had a fire in the late 1800s. It took a few days, but she remembered how she knew the story. A second-floor restaurant/bar in the West End had old newspaper clippings on the wall that chronicled the history of the district (which was mainly a warehouse and industrial area for decades that declined in the 1960s and 1970s before undergoing revitalization in the early 2000s). When Jones went to look for the clipping, it was gone. The owner said it had gone missing a few days before.

Jones also said they began noticing something else in the store. If their arms were filled when they went up a set of stairs to the storage area, somebody would try to kick out their knees from behind when they got to the third step. They wouldn't fall, but inevitability they would lose their balance. A medium would later tell her that a troll-like creature was living on the steps.

"It only happened when your arms were full," she said.

Jones and her assistant decided to keep the goings-on to themselves, but other things would soon happen that made it hard to keep the ghosts under wraps. People would come into the store and, after looking around, would begin asking questions about ghosts. Other people who were friends of Jones's and sensitive to paranormal experiences didn't like coming to see her there. There was something just not right. And sometimes Jones did little experiments. She would send people up the haunted steps with things in their hands. They would always come back to ask about what happened to their knees.

Then Jones hung a painting called "Habitat" that had the word "home" written on it. The lights above it began to flicker and fade. Every time she moved the painting, the lights it was under would flicker. Jones believes the ghosts were letting her know that this was their home and the store was invading. Still, the majority of the happenings were harmless. The two women even kidded one another about some of things that happened.

"It became sort of a joke to us after awhile," she said.

They soon learned more about the ghosts haunting the store. She told her young son to go sit in a chair at a red table on one side of the store. The three-year-old hesitated, and then told his mother that there was a young girl already sitting in the chair. Other people soon told Jones that the child was very kind and her name was either Mary or Marie. Her son, though, had a different name for Mary and the other odd things in the store. He called them "the pretties." He couldn't explain them, but every so often would tell his mother if the pretties were in the room. Jones soon had an experience herself. She closed the store for the night, but had to open up again later for a monthly tour of downtown artists' studios. She decided to take a nap on a futon. She woke up a little while later with the feeling that three people were standing over her. When she cleared her eyes, they were gone. Another person who later napped on the futon reported having a similar experience.

Aside from the female ghost, she believes the other ghosts were men. One was likely a teenager, and really didn't do much. The other was a grumpy older man, who was behind many of the tricks in the store, such as the flickering lights. He would also pull tissues out of boxes and flip them onto the floor. Several times Jones came to work and found her assistant hiding in the bathroom because of the odd things that happened. A person who was able to make contact with ghosts told Jones that the young girl kept the other two under wraps and tried to stop the pranks.

94

Jones also noticed that the ghosts had problems with religious symbols. An artist had hung a painting that had three crosses on it. That led to a series of odd actions. A cell phone sitting on a table turned on its speakerphone by itself and began playing a song about burning that was stored in its memory. Jones's husband was there at the time.

"I told him, 'See, this is what I've been telling you about,'" she said.

Jones quickly took the picture down and gave it back to the artist. She didn't want to get the ghosts more worked up than normal.

Eventually, in the autumn of 2007, Jones decided that she had had enough with ghosts and broken lights and malfunctioning computers. The ghosts needed to go. She contacted an "energy worker," which is somewhat like a medium or psychic, who could connect with ghosts and spirits. This particularly energy worker was skilled at cleaning out ghosts. Jones kept the venture to herself and arranged for a time when the energy worker could come by when the store was closed. The woman immediately told Jones that there were more than just three ghosts in her space. There were three vortexes as well. Two were high up on the ceiling in a corner of the room, while the third was located in the children's play area.

Vortexes are a mystery even to people who dabble in the supernatural, but they are generally believed to be connections to other places and are considered bad things. This bothered Jones, because in the last few week prior to the cleaning, her son had been reluctant to play in that area but wouldn't say why. Several other children also didn't like playing in the area.

The woman began talking to the spirits in the hope of getting them to cross over to the other side. She lit sage and muldovite candles, which are supposed to help clear out unwanted spirits. The woman also closed the vortexes by using prayers and the like. Jones watched the procedure with some curiosity. She wanted the ghosts gone, but also felt badly about it because the ghosts had been there first.

The cleaning ended up drawing some unusual onlookers, as other ghosts were lining up to see if they could be crossed over as well. During the process, Jones said she felt something near her neck. The energy worker told her there was a good reason for that, because a man in a Confederate soldier's uniform was holding a bayonet to her throat. He had changed his mind about crossing over, and wanted to stay. Jones said it was scary to hear that, but that she was in no real danger. He eventually crossed with no problems.

The woman told Jones that downtown Greenville was teeming with countless numbers of ghosts and specters. One that the energy worker mentioned is "Bloody Bill" Bates, a Tory officer responsible for several brutal massacres in the Upstate during the Revolutionary War. He fled Greenville after the war, but came back during a horse raid. Caught and recognized for his misdeeds during the war, he was killed before going to trial. It is said that his body was buried in a dirt lot on Main Street near where the present-day City Hall is located. The massive Springwood Cemetery also is located downtown. Jones said there are some energy workers who refuse to go to downtown Greenville because there is so much paranormal activity that has accumulated over the decades.

"It's just too much for them," Jones said.

The woman eventually finished, and said the building was now clean. Jones was relieved, and wondered how people who had seen the ghosts would react. The first was her son. He came running into the store after school and immediately stopped as he looked into the children's area. He said, "The monster's gone." That unnerved Jones, but she explained to him that the "pretties" and everyone else were gone after he asked what had happened to them.

"If he had been seeing a monster, I wish he had told me earlier and I would have cleaned out the ghosts," she said.

Other people soon came in, and they said the store and design area seemed more healthy and that whatever had manifested itself in the store was now gone. Many of these were the

96

same people who had described having odd feelings in there in the past, and who had refused to stay in the store for extended periods of time. None of them knew what she had done, and were relieved to later learn that she had safely cleaned out the spirits. The woman who cleaned her space of the ghosts and vortexes came by a few months later and said the building was still clear.

But best of all, Jones joked, was that she stopped having computer problems. Not a single crash or virus or unexplained failure.

"Though, I have to admit I miss them a little," she said. "I felt very, very sad for them, but it was time."

# What Goes Thump in the Night?
## Strange Sounds and Sights from an Anderson Home

Renee Elders (not her real name) didn't believe in ghosts. Never got the visceral kick out of hearing ghost stories around the campfire. Never spent money on going to the movies to watch a horror film, and usually turned the channel if she saw one on television. They were just too boring, she said.

"I never got into that joy of being scared," she said. "It wasn't for me."

It may still not bring joy, but the divorced mother of three can never say again that ghost stories are boring, not after living in a bungalow near downtown Anderson for almost two years. There were strange noises at night. Glasses and dishes breaking by themselves. And finally the vision of someone—or something—that made her flee the house in terror.

Elders first moved into the house in 1993 because it was relatively cheap and in a quiet neighborhood where she and her kids could walk downtown or to the parks on the weekend. Neither the previous tenants nor the owners had mentioned anything about past haunts or spectral experiences, but her kids told her they were immediately uneasy in the new house.

"The first night there, they kept saying they felt someone else was in the house," she said. "I figured they were just being silly because they were in a new place."

Her daughters, who were teens at the time, carried flashlights around most of the night checking closets and the crawl space in the attic. She scolded them for trying to scare their little brother, and ordered them to bed for the night. She finally slumped into her own room a little after midnight. That is when she heard what sounded like a ball slowing bouncing down a flight of stairs. Her first thought was that a wayward ball had fallen down the steps—a common occurrence at her old house—until she realized there were no steps inside the house. She shot up in bed and went into the living room, but saw nothing out of the ordinary. She reasoned she had imagined the noise.

The next few days were relatively ordinary as she unpacked boxes and set up her new home. Her daughters stopped mentioning the odd feelings and she forgot about the weird thumping noise from that first night—that is, until her son came crawling into her bed around 3 a.m. complaining about hearing thumping in the house. The boy quickly curled up into an easy slumber, but Elders was frozen wide awake. She kept listening to see if she could hear the noises as well. There was nothing and eventually she dozed off.

In the morning, she awoke to find her son was gone and again she thought maybe she had dreamed it. She found the boy in the kitchen eating a bowl of cereal and asked him how he was doing. The boy, who was around seven, said he was fine. She asked about what drove him from his bed, and he said it sounded like someone was bouncing a tiny ball. Elders said it was the house settling and not to worry about it. However, she made a mental note to talk to her daughters when they got up. She asked the older daughter about the sound when the other two had gone out to play. The daughter said she had heard nothing and swore she was not playing a trick on her brother. Later she questioned the younger girl alone, and she said the same thing. But Elders added that the daughter still didn't like the house. She said it felt like someone was always looking over her shoulder just out of sight.

"She got really emotional and said it was scaring her," Elders said. "She was really scared by it. She said she wanted to move."

Elders was not sure what to do next. Two of her children had been scared by something in the house, but she wasn't sure if this was anxiety from the move or some kind of prank being pulled by the kids. Her own fears soon lessened as nothing out of the ordinary happened for the next few weeks, but then came the first of what she and her kids started to call "thump weeks."

It started on Sunday. The kids were playing in the backyard and she was in the kitchen cooking some baked macaroni and cheese for dinner. She could see them running around out back when she was startled to hear something in the living room. It sounded like someone was bouncing a ball off the wall. She ran into the room and nothing was there. She went to the front door to check if it was still locked, but as soon as her hand reached the brass knob she heard a bouncing noise in the kitchen. She spun around, but nothing was there and she could see the kids through one of the windows.

"I don't know why, but I was very scared," she said. "I called the kids into the house to get ready for dinner. I didn't want to be alone."

Dinner went normally, and the family sat down in the living room to watch television. That is when they heard the bouncing noise come from Elders's room in the back of the house. All four of them just froze and turned their heads toward room. The noise was very faint, but Elders forced herself to walk back there. She peaked into the room and flicked on the light switch. As soon as the lamp turned on, the noise stopped. Her older daughter came behind her and asked what was going on. Elders just shook her head slightly and said it was the wind. The teen raised her eyebrow in incredulous disbelief, but before either could continue the discussion a thumping noise came from the front bedroom. Elders raced past her daughter, saw her two other kids kneeling on the couch with their mouths agape and staring at the door, and went to the bedroom. She flung open the door and the noises stopped.

"The kids were all kind of crying, so I said, 'Let's go get some ice cream,' and hustled them out the door," she said. "We were gone for a few hours and I called the landlord from a pay phone to say I thought there was some kind of rodent in the walls."

The landlord agreed to send someone over to look at the house and footed the bill for the family to spend the night in a motel. Elders and the kids returned to the home in the morning and met with the landlord. There was no sign of a squirrel, rat, mouse, or anything in the house, and he said it likely was just the house settling. Elders didn't want to say she thought it was a ghost, but at that point she was running out of answers. The thumps continued for the next few days. Sometimes all four heard the noise, sometimes it was just one or two of them. The events went from being scary to being annoying to being just part of life in the house.

After five days, though, the thumps stopped and didn't happen again for months, she said. They would come back at intervals after that. It would start on a Sunday and go to about Thursday, and then go silent again for months. The kids joked about living in a haunted house, but would still run to their mom's room when the thumps would start again.

"It sounds strange, but we just sort of lived with it. The house was haunted and there was nothing we could do about it," she said.

An event around Christmas that year started to make Elders think more about what was going on. Some friends were coming over and she started to get some plates down off a shelf. The first one she grabbed was broken right down the middle. Putting it to the side, she reached for a second one. It also was cracked right down the middle and fell apart in her hands. She nudged the stack, and the remaining plates all seemed to collapse in front of her. She called in her kids and asked if one of them had broken the plates. They all said it wasn't them.

"I can usually tell if my kids are lying, and I felt they were being honest," she recalled.

She put the broken plates in the trash and placed some other plates as well as some wine glasses on the countertop. She didn't think about the weird thumps and rationalized that they were old plates and maybe the cupboard was too dry or damp for dishes. Her friends arrived and she went to greet them at the door. She called the kids out of their rooms and invited everyone into the kitchen to get some food.

"I got into the kitchen and saw that all of the wine glasses had been cracked," she said. "They were all standing, but they looked like spiderwebs they were so cracked."

Elders was stunned and told her friends about the broken plates. Her kids then mentioned "thump weeks" and the time they stayed in a hotel. All of her friends said they would have left immediately, but Elders said she was going to bill the ghost for damages first. They all laughed about it, but for the first time since the first "thump week" Elders felt uncomfortable in the house. She tried to do some research on the house, but couldn't find anything that would make her think something in the home's history had anything to do with the odd events. No murders. No suicides. No violence. She decided against contacting a psychic or a medium because she didn't want the attention. The kids didn't seem to be overly scared either, so she decided to stick it out for a few more months.

However, things changed in June. Her younger daughter came into her room around 3 a.m. one night and said she had had a nightmare. She told her mother that she dreamed a man had come into her room and sat at the edge of the bed. He was very dark skinned and looked angry. Elders consoled her that it was just a dream and let her sleep in bed with her. The next morning the girl said it was scary because the dream had seemed so real. Elders asked the girl not to say anything to her siblings. Even though they had grown accustomed to the thumps, she didn't want them to get scared by something else. But a day afterward, her oldest daughter came to her and described a "crazy" dream about a dark-skinned man with a sinister smile. Elders just stopped in her tracks.

"That scared me a lot. I immediately felt those two were connected," she said. "I didn't tell my daughter that, but I was suddenly very nervous."

The next night would prove the clincher. Elders got home from work and none of the lights were on, which wasn't that surprising in the summer because her kids were out playing with friends. She opened the front door and looked right into the kitchen. She saw what looked like a man sitting at the table. His face turned up toward her. He was very dark skinned and had a very sinister smile. The image lasted about five seconds and simply vanished in a haze before Elders could react to a possible intruder. She stared at the kitchen for a few more seconds, almost frozen in fear, and then walked back out the front door. She drove to get her kids, then went to her mother's house.

"I wasn't going to spend another night there," she said. "Whatever my girls saw was definitely not a dream because I saw it."

Elders never re-entered the home. She had friends and family remove her belongings. She wasn't sure if they believed her story, but they could tell she was unnerved by something in the house. She soon found a new place to live on the other side of town. It wasn't as big as her last place, she said, but at least no ghost showed up in the kitchen.

"My kids still drive by that house and tell me it's still there," she said. "Not me. I avoid that street."

# Talking with the Other Side
## A Recounting of Some Very Chilling Recordings in Greenville

I never thought the most scared I would get while researching an Upstate ghost story would be while sitting around a circular kitchen table with a cat purring at my feet and a big jar filled with Oreo cookies at my shoulder, but that is what happened when I visited Tom Smith (an alias) in Travelers Rest.

Smith had a collection of EVPs, photos, and a video of orbs, faces, and other supernatural inklings that ran a chill up and down my back. A true skeptic might say that Smith was trying to pull a hoax by calling a person working on a ghost book to show him some evidence, but I sought him out after somebody told me about his large collection of supernatural finds. And it was an amazing collection. Numerous pictures of red, green, and bright white orbs. A skull-like face in the back of another photo. A child's face peaking out of the corner of a television screen. On video, there was a head-like subject that pops out of nowhere, floats around the room, makes a sharp turn, and vanishes. Then there were the EVPs—voices captured on audio equipment that were not heard by human ears when the recordings were made. Some threatened Smith and his family. One asked Smith to dig up his grave. Others told him what they missed about being alive. They have tapped his shoulders and head. Even his family has seen things that couldn't be explained, such as a floating torso. He even captured an image of a floating skull at his sister's house. For Smith, it has opened up avenues into a spirit world that he always believed existed, but now gets to see up close way too much.

Smith was born in Florida and raised Catholic. His family moved to western North Carolina in the early 1970s and he grew up hearing the numerous ghost stories of the mountain region. However, he never really experienced anything first-hand until he was in a truck accident in the late 1990s. He almost lost his life, and he experienced the terrifying vision of seeing his life flash before his eyes. That made him believe there was more than just death awaiting him.

"I can't really explain it," he said. "It all happened in a split second."

When Smith recovered, he started noticing things in his peripheral vision. Strange objects and blurs that would dart just out of sight. The photos he took would have glowing objects in them. He heard people call his name when no one else was there. He started to study theories on the paranormal. He found that many psychics and paranormalists believe there is the earthly plane and around it there is an astral plane. People who have experienced being close to death are often able to see into that other plane.

The majority of ghosts, a term that Smith tries to avoid (he prefers to call them entities, spirits, or people), are angry about what has happened to them. They were murdered or committed suicide. They died in an accident or left people behind. They are disgruntled because they are stuck in a sort of limbo. They can't contact their loved ones, but they can't escape the mortal world. Most don't want to communicate with the living, but there is a small percentage who do. Unfortunately, they don't always have the energy or the memory to say what they want to say. They tend to feed off the energy of living people. If a person is happy and content, then the spirits around them will act the same way. A negative person will cause negative actions. That is why many paranormalists believe that "poltergeist" activity normally erupts in homes where a child is going through puberty. The more energy a person has, the more a ghost will be drawn to them.

"It really is a battle between good and evil," Smith said. "Light attracts light. Dark attracts dark."

And with that come repercussions. Smith said the supernatural cannot be treated lightly. There are a lot bad spirits and even demons that want to take over people's lives, he said. People can easily get so caught up with looking for ghosts and specters that they don't realize they are being drawn into something they can't understand. That has happened to Smith on several occasions.

It was a dark spirit that Smith first encountered after his accident. He was in bed and heard banging coming from a bathroom. When he went in, all of the cabinet doors were open. He shut them, but a few minutes later he heard the thuds again. When he returned to the room, the doors were open again.

That went on for about a week, then one night he heard a buzzing noise coming from the attic. This was in the middle of the winter and it was about 12 degrees outside, and not much warmer in the attic. He hurried his way up a set of stairs to see if he could figure out what was going on. Swinging open the door, he immediately turned his gaze toward the windows at the opposite end of the room, where the sound was coming from. A swarm of flies was covering in the windows.

The flies' writhing winged bodies formed an almost completely black curtain over the glass. He watched for a second and wondered how on earth the flies got there, then shut the door and placed an overnight call to an exterminator. However, when the exterminator got there the next morning, they found only two dead flies on the carpet. They looked for ways that the rest of the flying insects could have escaped, but never found anything. The exterminator said there was no earthly way so many flies could be buzzing around in such cold weather. Smith soon learned this was a sign of a demonic presence, and he got the house blessed. That ended much of the odd noises.

He moved to southern Greenville County around 2002, and that is when his real journey into understanding the supernatural began. He took a job working third shift, but his body was having trouble adjusting to the new sleep schedule. One night when he wasn't working, he lulled into somewhat of a daydream. He was lying on a purple couch and looked over at the love seat and saw a man holding his young daughter on his lap. They were playing innocently. He glanced over at the television and then looked back at the man and his daughter. The man was now choking the child. Smith got up and started to do anything to break the man's grip. As soon as he got the man off his daughter, he woke up back on the couch in a scream.

Scared and confused, Smith checked on his daughter, who was sleeping soundly. For the rest of the week, he had a recurring dream that he was in an abandoned house somewhat akin to the farmhouse in the original *Night of the Living Dead,* a movie that scared him greatly when he was young. The man would come to him in the house and say, "You're not going to win."

It was around then that Smith began taking some photos behind his house. Like many of his photos, they were filled with orbs. They would be in the trees and around his family members. Smith believes that the orbs are the energy left over from a spirit and cites Albert Einstein's theory that raw energy is circular in form. As he looked at the developed photos, he noticed something in one of the windows of his home. It appeared to be a face looking out. It was the face of the man he had seen in his dreams. He was shocked, but not surprised, because of all he had seen.

A short while later, he was watching a movie one night when he heard a strange popping noise coming from the television. He decided to take some pictures. One of the snapshots showed what appeared to be a boy's face peaking through the television screen. Behind him was a very sinister looking man. Smith has theorized that the sinister man is the spirit that is holding all of the other entities to the property. He learned this by doing EVPs in the home, which he started shortly after taking the pictures.

He played me a few dozen of the several hundred that he collected inside the home. One of the more scary ones was a person identifying himself as "John." This spirit told Smith that he was buried in the backyard and gave precise directions on where to dig. Smith, though, consulted other paranormal investigators over the Internet, who warned him that John likely wasn't friendly and actually was the evil spirit in the house. The presence was trying to lure Smith into doing his bidding.

Around the same time, Smith also began to feel an urge to buy a Ouija board. He mentioned it in passing to his mother, who responded that that was odd. Just the day before she had been going through some old photos and found one that contained a Ouija board from the early 1970s, which his sisters had destroyed after some very scary experiences. Smith took that as a warning sign not to bring a Ouija board into his home. He had bought one, but smashed it into about twenty pieces in his garage after his wife said she didn't want it in the house. Needless to say, he never tried to dig up the grave.

"There is no such thing as coincidence or déjà vu," Smith said. "I've learned to trust my gut feeling when dealing with these entities."

It is somewhat easy to get entranced by hearing the recordings, he said, which is why he started to do so many of them. Smith played back for me some of the earliest contacts he made. I found it unsettling to hear the voices myself. He uses a radio or television turned down low to help focus the spirit's energy. He asks a question or two, waits a minute, and then rewinds. If he gets an answer, he tries to get the spirit into a conversation. The first night he simply asked if there was anyone there, and a breath-like "me" could be heard. When he asked for a name, a woman's voice answered "Tracey." He kept at it. During the course of the night, he got more names and one that simply moaned as if in pain. Soon, though, one spirit became belligerent and began a violent blue streak of cursing aimed at Smith, which made him stop. However, Smith wanted to know who was cursing at him and went through the same procedure the next night. A woman's voice identified herself as Keirdon. When he asked if she was the one who had been rude the night before, the voice answered, "You're going to die. You won't take them for granted."

That bothered Smith greatly, and the spirit refused to answer anything else. More ghosts, though, would soon pop up. Smith said on a normal night it becomes like a McDonald's drive-through window as spirits line up to talk. Some would call out his name. Others began to answer questions even before Smith had finished speaking. Smith theorized that this was due to the spirit world working at a much faster speed than the earthly plane. He suspects that this is a major reason most people never catch more than just a glimpse of something or that photos catch mostly blurs. He also said they know a lot about the people who are trying to contact them. Many will only talk when Smith says out loud that he is about to stop recording. For some reason, the ghosts have learned that Smith is able to contact them and have started to flock to him. He can even do EVPs while driving his truck and pick up answers.

"They are aware of what is going on in our world," he said.

And while some of the spirits have been scary and threatening, others have caused Smith sadness. One voice could be heard gasping, "I'm here, I'm right here." Smith asked if there was anything he could do for the spirit. The entity could be heard coughing and then stated, "As if you care." Around the same time, Smith said he felt a cool, damp feeling envelop him. He believed the spirit in question may have died from cancer or another serious ailment. Smith later tried to apologize to the entity, but could never again get him to speak. Another time he asked the spirits what they missed the most about the living world. After a few seconds, one voice could be heard whispering ,"My dad." It was followed by another voice stating, "Being outdoors."

109

Smith also has tried to figure out how old some of the spirits are. He once asked if any of the spirits had ever seen *The Twilight Zone*. There were a couple of nos, and then a voice stating, "I saw it." Another ghost would later tell Smith that he died in 1890, but it hadn't felt like that much time had passed. Another spirit said she was there to watch over Smith's family. Another said it was possible that the spirits might follow them when they moved.

Smith also learned to ask that any spirits that might answer him be positive and that angry or evil spirits stay away. However, the ghosts didn't always hold to the rule of being positive. One could be heard to say in a raspy voice, "Tom, your time has come." Another time he asked into the recorder if there was anything he could do to help the spirits. A gravelly voice could be heard answering, "Kill her, kill her." That one deeply bothered Smith, and his arms got goose bumps on them when he played the audio for me again, years after it had been made. He was not sure who the spirit wanted killed, but luckily he never heard from that being again.

Despite the scares and the massive amount of contacts, one of the main things he has tried to do is to get the spirits to be more specific. He often asks them to speak directly into his recorder or to manifest themselves. Other times he asks them to tap his shoulder. Many times voices could be heard saying yes to these requests, but the spirits seldom followed through. Smith said it is best to be respectful when trying to contact the other plane, because that helps keep encounters positive.

He wasn't the only person to experience odd things in the home. One morning, he heard his wife, Mary, scream from the garage. He ran into the room to see if she was all right and found her standing on the steps. He asked what had happened. She said she had seen a man's torso floating near the cars. Another time she had a feeling that someone was standing behind her in the bathroom. After about six months of living in the southern Greenville County home, the Smiths brought in a priest to bless the home. And when they moved to a new home in Travelers Rest, which was more for convenience than to escape the ghosts, they did the same thing.

"It's about peace of mind," he said. "I think it's just a good thing to do."

However, that did not diminish Smith's interactions with the spirit world. He took a picture in his sister's house, and there above the bed was the outline of a grisly human skull with a long forehead, wide eye sockets, and a sinister smile. His family's three cats will act strange—even by feline standards. One will run around the house as if being chased and won't stop until it collapses in exhaustion, he said. Smith also showed me a video that he had taken in his new home just a few days before I interviewed him. He took it in a bedroom, and asked questions to the spirits just as he had with audio equipment. At least three times, a white flickering light could be seen zipping along the edges of the frame. Smith would pan from one side of the room to another and stop periodically. As the viewer stopped over some paintings on the wall, a head-like object appeared out of nowhere and floated in front of the paintings. It moved maybe about two feet before abruptly shifting gears and floating back in the direction it had started out from. It vanished just as quickly as it had appeared. In a video from another room, a voice could be heard saying, "Tom, what's in your hand."

While Smith has been able to break the habit of searching for spirits daily, the other side hasn't tired of getting in touch with him. If he doesn't do an audio or video recording for a while, the spirits let him know they are around. One way is by flipping his cell phone on a table when no one is around. This happened for about a week straight before Smith did some recordings. The flipping then stopped.

"The thing about paranormal research is that it is all theory," he said. "There are no set scientific ways of going about it. One person may say I am doing it wrong, but this is what has worked for me."

And while he had a few scary moments—the flies at the window, the vision of his daughter, and the strange request to kill come to mind—he mostly accepts what happens and even finds some solace in it. The video and the recordings show him that death isn't the end.

"I used to fear death," he said. "Now I know there is more out there."

# Inside a Haunted House Investigation
## Finding Out What Lurks in a House in Piedmont

I could hardly believe the email that had binged in my inbox. It was from the South Carolina Paranormal Research and Investigations president, asking if I wanted to observe one of their investigations of a haunted house in the little Anderson County town of Piedmont. Over the course of my looking for haunted places in numerous states, this was the first time that a ghost hunting group was giving me the opportunity to check out an investigation up close, and maybe see something that couldn't be unexplained. I have often stated that I have no ability to see, speak to, or hear firsthand anything from the other side, and I was intrigued to be around people who actively experience such things.

I showed up at the one-story white house around 2 p.m. to talk to some of the team members and learn about the house. The homeowner said there had been a lot of odd things since she, her husband, and their daughter had moved in about six years before. Some of them were little experiences, such as flickering lights, a computer that shuts downs and restarts by itself several times a week, and strange noises. She also said the brass pull chain hanging from the living room ceiling fan would sometimes jangle when there was no movement in the room. Other things were much more frightening.

Shortly after moving into the house, her husband was taking a shower while getting ready for work. When he pulled back the curtain, he saw a young woman staring back at him in the mirror. He reflexively looked behind himself, and then turned back to look at the mirror. The young woman was gone. He told his wife about it that day, and they both wondered what it might have been. The homeowner soon saw animals running across the floors. The odd thing was that they were animals of hers that had died years before. One night she felt someone pull the covers, and when she looked up she could feel a presence sitting at the edge of the bed. There is also a black and gold music box that moves around the house when no one is there. One of the more frightening events was when she came home one day and her neighbor hailed her down. The neighbor said she had seen a woman in period dress floating around in the front yard. The being then floated up the steps to the front porch and vanished through the front door.

The haunting soon escalated. Her daughter started to refuse to sleep in her own bed. She said she didn't feel comfortable in her bedroom at the back of the house and would do anything she could to stay out of the room at night. The young girl told her mother she felt scared in the room. One night she woke up her mother and said she felt like somebody had run a finger down her back.

"That was the first thing that really spooked me," she said.

As far as the homeowner can tell, there have been no tragic events on the property, such as a murder or suicide, but she believes the land may have been used by Native Americans. She has found shamans' stones and arrowheads while digging in her garden over the years. One of the rocks shows a little pictograph of a man fishing and the sun shining overhead. She also believes one of the ghosts may be her grandfather.

The unexplained events in the house come and go, but they seemed to escalate after she started doing work with SCPRAI. After a few months, she invited the team to investigate her home. Team members began showing up in mid-afternoon to talk and share ghost stories and to learn more about the home. At one point, I saw the homeowner lean over to a woman who has a history of seeing unexplained things and heard her say that she had just seen something move in a mirror in one the bedrooms. The psychic just nodded. I have to admit, that sent a chill up and down my spine.

I noticed that many of the ghost hunters shared many of the same backgrounds. They had been seeing and hearing things that couldn't be explained for most of their lives. They joined SCPRAI because they wanted the opportunity to share their findings with others. It was a very close group that was not afraid to cut up on each other while recounting some of their past investigations and each other's foibles. That helped ease my trepidation a little, as I felt I was more at a party for old friends than at a haunted house. They even critiqued the glut of "paranormal" shows that were playing on cable television, which led to some funny discussions about the reality of some of the shows. That ease, though, would slip as the time for the actual investigation drew closer.

The investigation would start just after sundown. Shelley Armstrong, the group's founder, said that there are several reasons they hold off on starting investigations until sundown. One is that pictures taken at night tend to show more spectral activity than ones taken when there is a lot of light. The second reason is that many of the homes they have investigated tend to have most of their activity at night. And third, she somewhat joked, is that people expect to see ghost hunters work more at night. Armstrong laid out several metal attaché cases filled with all kinds of paranormal equipment, including infrared cameras, electromagnetic sensors, regular cameras, video recorders, ultraviolet flashlights, divining rods, and temperature meters. The tools are essential when trying to explain the unexplained, she said.

Armstrong said that the group would be split up into several teams and each assigned a room to investigate. After about thirty minutes, the teams would switch rooms but wouldn't talk about what they had seen or heard. In addition, the power to the house would be turned off to prevent the electricity's creating any problems with the equipment. That way, if something turns on in the house during the investigation, it can be credited to the presence of a ghost rather than to a power surge. Armstrong also tells people to be as quiet as possible—but if they must talk, not to whisper and always to say who they are when they are talking. This is done to help cut down on false readings. They don't want a group in one room to pick up sounds from team members in other rooms and think they are ghosts.

Soon, the sun started to set, and the group of investigators—thirteen in all—started to talk less. A group of Wofford College students were there working on a documentary. They got a little antsy when one of them reported that a flashlight he had just purchased was not working. The lithium battery drained while they were in the house. Another's truck alarm system went off for no reason. Myself, I have to admit I was a little nervous. I was going to stay in the kitchen taking notes as the groups went from room to room. Some team members went through the rooms taking temperature readings and looking for electrical hot spots. Others divvied up the rest of the equipment and put cassette tapes in their recorders. Shortly after 6 p.m., the owner turned off the power to the house. The home grew silent as the teams went into the various rooms and shut the doors. At first, the only noise I could hear was the tick-tock of a battery-powered clock on the walk. The owner of the house said, "Come on out ghosties, come on out." My heart started to pound a little bit faster in anticipation.

I soon heard the people in the various rooms asking questions aloud. While they don't expect to hear anything immediately, they hope that their recording equipment will pick up something they can hear when they play it back. Some of their questions included, What is your name? Do you know the people in this house? When did you die? How many spirits are there? Are you an earthbound spirit? Are you following somebody at the house tonight? Did you live on this spot? It was interesting to hear the voices coming from the other rooms as

116

the investigators found creative ways to ask questions of the other side.

The house was incredibly dark, and the only illumination was from the flash of cameras and the headlights of cars as people drove down the road. All of a sudden, there was a commotion in the front room. A flashlight belonging to the owner turned on by itself. That sent several people chattering about it while the homeowner explained into the recorder what had just happened. Armstrong used a special blue light to help the homeowner focus some photographs. The blue light is supposed to provide a clearer picture and cut down on accidental shadows and lights that could be mistaken for orbs.

Other odd noises were easily explained. An odd dripping noise was the ice cubes in some plastic cups melting. A banging noise from the pantry was a cat jumping on the washing machine. In the distance, some dogs could be heard barking.

At one point, the homeowner asked Armstrong if she'd just felt anything? Armstrong said she had just seen what looked like fingers play along the front window. The homeowner said she had asked because she felt what seemed like a cold chill behind her. Armstrong then reported she felt like she was having a panic attack and that it was something she had never felt in a house before. Armstrong soon calmed herself, but things then got a little more spooky.

The homeowner asked out loud if the spirit was her grandfather. A loud thump came from one of the walls inside the room. And another man in the room said he saw what appeared to be a black swoosh zoom across the room. The trio of ghost hunters talked excitedly about this latest occurrence, and wondered if the thump might have been made by one of the teams in the other rooms. Armstrong then again saw the mysterious fingers flicker across the front window. She asked me if I had seen anything. I said I hadn't, but of course I had been staring intently in my lap as I scribbled down notes on a white legal pad. I paid more attention to the window after that, but neither Armstrong nor I saw anything more.

After the teams switched rooms, Armstrong and the homeowner went outside to investigate what might have caused the movement along the windows. A tree blowing in the breeze?. Headlights from a car? An actual person walking by? Maybe someone on the road? Remember, the homeowner's neighbor had once seen a person in period dress floating around in the front yard. Could this visitor have returned that night? The movement along the windows couldn't have been made from the road because the shadow of someone walking along there didn't go that far during the night. The headlights on the cars that drove down the narrow road never got close enough to the house to cast a shadow, either. Neither Armstrong nor any of the rest of the team could explain it. A little while later, several people who were in the house reported seeing a very strange blue glow in several of the rooms. Not surprisingly, this caused a lot of commotion.

There were few other scares or oddities during the night, and a day later it was time to review the tapes and videos. Armstrong said unfortunately they were unable to get any photos or video of the blue light. However, they were able to get some shots of mysterious orbs in their photographs. They also recorded what Armstrong classified as low-level EVPs, the unexplained noises that followed some of the questions asked by the teams. Myself, well I left with my streak intact. I hadn't experiencing anything out of the ordinary at all.